THE GREAT PROVIDER

JENNY EDWARDS

BALBOA.
PRESS

A DIVISION OF HAY HOUSE

Balboa Press books may be ordered through booksellers or by contacting:

Balboa Press
A Division of Hay House
1663 Liberty Drive
Bloomington, IN 47403
www.balboapress.com.au
1 (877) 407-4847

Printed in the United States of America.

ISBN: 978-1-4525-2652-2 (sc)
ISBN: 978-1-4525-2653-9 (e)

Balboa Press rev. date: 11/18/2014

Jessie & Ernest Johns (as children)

Sarah Johns & James (Her son-Dads Brother)

Editorial

This is a true biographical story. Beginning in 1886 and following the lives of two sets of grandparents and following through to the children that now have their own story to tell.

To the memory of my dear Dad
with special thanks to my Mum

Dedicated to My Four sons Robert,
Trevor, Shaun & Raymond who
I am immensely Proud of.
Love Moma

JENNY

PART ONE

THE BEGINNING

Like the sands of time, so are the days of our lives. The sands of time in this story begin to flow in 1886. Ada Emily Beatrice Norman was born that year, born into a world far removed from the fast pace we know today. She was born before many inventions, and a far cry from World Wars. Brought up in a Victorian family, dresses reached the floor and met the buttoned boots, not an inch of flesh would show. An elegant time, the horse bus transported you to your destination.

In the three hundred years between the Norman Conquest and the death of the Black Prince in 1371, Plymouth grew to become the fourth town in England in size and one of its most important ports;

Ada was born in Plymouth, her early life remains unknown and untalked about, but we know that she grew into a beautiful young woman with fine skin and hair. Her company was sought after by the opposite sex, but her initial choice of a man was to prove tragic. She was carrying her first child, a boy, when the telegram arrived to announce that the man she intended to marry, who was the father of her child, was killed in action. The words from the war office simply conveyed that this child would never know its father.

Picture from after the WW1

The 1914 war when it came in August, was not the brief and glorious adventure they had been led to expect, and the lives of everyone, even those far from the mud of Flanders became bogged down in the grinding conflict that followed. Familys all over were to suffer the sad receipt of a telegram with the printed words KILLED IN ACTION.

At the same time in our story in another area of Plymouth, Devon, another woman, Sarah Jane Johns (nee Sloman) was raising a large family after marrying James Johns, better known to everyone as Jimmy. She also received a similar telegram. Her son of nineteen years, Jimmy Johns Jnr. was shot through the head as he tried to climb clear of a trench, during the thick of the fighting. When she received the news, Sarah, a fine looking woman with striking features, had a full head of dark hair, she took to her bed clutching the telegram tight to her chest. When she awoke much later, her fine tresses were grey. Tragedy had robbed her of her youth.

These two women, Sarah Johns and Ada Norman had never met, they lived separate lives in the same town. In their own way they produced the story I am about to tell. A true story of life, love, anguish, pain and laughter.

THE STORY BEGINS

Picture a pretty little harbour, just up the coast from Plymouth. Brixham had its fair share of small fishermans cottages and wooden fishing boats. The port survived on the industry. The year is 1888, the boats bobbed about in the bay saucily challenging the icy winter winds.

In one of the little cottages, William George Westlake was born on the night of 29th November 1888. He was the baby who would grow into manhood and propose to Ada, who lost her first love in the war. The child she gave birth too, Stanley Norman, was three years old at the time they first set eyes on each other, he fell for the beautiful Ada and she accepted his proposal of marriage. William Westlake was a seaman who had been sent to sea by his father at the tender age of eleven. He sailed the great tall ships. The long haul to India and Africa around the Cape with the winds beating mercilessly against the big wooden ships, sculptured him into a hard determined man. He survived each long dangerous trip to return to his dear wife, who produced a child after each shore leave.

At the time of their marriage little Stanley was three years old. The first child born of their union was a girl, Beatrice (Beattie). The second child, also a girl was named Jessie Emily. The third child yet another girl, was named Edna. She was just two years and four months old when another baby was on its way. Could William have the son he yearned for this time. He had returned from a journey to India when the child was conceived, the year was now 1916. Ada was still a young woman of twenty nine and her husband two years younger at twenty seven when the woman of this story was born to them. Her birth was late December, 29th December 1916, the child, another girl, weighed a hefty 10lbs. 8oz. a nice comfortable start to a life that held very few treats in those times.

Phylis Lillian Westlake was born in the same Victoria Buildings in Harwell Street, Portland Square, where her mother and grandmother lived. She was born in a back bedroom, the doctors visits cost tuppence a time, and Ada already owed the doctor plenty for past visits, so she struggled bravely and delivered her baby with the help of other women who occupied flats in the buildings.

With a husband away at sea for long periods of time, a woman with five children had her work cut out.
The buildings were a collection of eight flats that were reached by walking through an arched passageway that was always dark, damp and dismal, this opened out into a communal courtyard where everything took place. Women gathered on Monday mornings armed with tin baths, scrubbing boards (Dollyboards) and huge cakes of soap, ready to do the family wash.
Ada would dress for the occasion covering her ample frame with a large apron made from sacking.

Whilst the cauldron bubbled away above the fire in the flat cooking six penneth of meat and two penneth of veg, Ada would spend all day Monday which was 'Wash-Day', dressed in an old sack apron to protect her clothes, and with her old mans boots on she would wash and scrub the clothes, with the sound of laughter and children's noise around in the courtyard. The air was full of peace after the end of the first world war. The women chattered amongst themselves, filling lines full of clothes blowing in the warm sunshine.

1920

Time moved on. Phylis was three years old when she was enrolled in the State School to learn her three 'R's reading - riting - rithmetic. She would return home after the long day to watch as her mother fed the latest arrival. This baby was so welcome, because it was a boy. George was the baby that broke the pattern of all the girls. Pregnancy was never discussed at home, your mother just wore a bigger apron to conceal her changing shape, so it was no surprise when just a year later in 1921, Ada produced another boy. This child was a sad reminder of what can go wrong. Baby Gerald was born with a very enlarged head, he was brain deformed and both ears had been damaged by severe birth complications.

The house was quiet, there was no celebrating. They quickly named the child Gerald, he sadly died a week later. Phylis remembered seeing his small still body laid out in a large shoe box. With tiny hands she reached up to the top of the dresser towering above her, pulled herself up and peeked into the shoe box. She was five and a half at the time.

1922

It had been a long hot summer, full of wash days and ironing days, a feat in itself with huge heavy irons heated on the shelf of the open fire, and tested for temperature with spittle - if it sizzled it was hot enough. A heavy blanket was thrown across the table, covered by an old sheet which bore scorch marks made from previous ironing days. Hours of pressing white pinafores began.

With the tragedy of the previous year's loss well behind her and the family growing away, Beattie, Jessie and Edna as young women out dancing and enjoying the attentions of young men. Ada, their mother became the butt of their jokes by becoming pregnant yet again. Beattie was working in the laundry of the City Hospital (now Freedom Fields). Jessie was 'In-Service' for a very nice family, Mr and Mrs Kitto who had a large house on Citadel Road, The Hoe. In Plymouth. They treasured Jessie's services. The two girls were not amused when their mother got pregnant at such an age! Ada was thirty six years old when the twins arrived without ceremony, so now the family was increased by two more mouths to feed in the form of Thomas and Alfred, that made nine.

To complete Ada's part in our story we leap to 1929. By then Ada had respectfully reared eight children, nine if you count the baby she sadly lost. She had done this almost single handedly, caring for her own bedridden mother as well. When at fourty three she discovered she was about to bear another child. Roy Westlake was born March 17th 1929. Ada had a rough time, she was ill with the birth of Roy Eric. He was a small sickly baby, he survived to be a weak frail boy with a wonderful sense of humour, he would think up lots of ways to keep his elder sisters busy amusing him.

Roy was so weak at one stage that he had to be lifted outside and put in a chair to enjoy the sunshine, but he was still too weak to raise his little arms.

Even his ill health in childhood did not prevent him from being an excellent scholar, he went on to pass his eleven plus exam with the highest of marks, and after grammar school his father enrolled him in the Navy to go to sea just like he had done with all the boys of the family, they had no choice in the matter. No one in those days was ever consulted on how they viewed their future. It was decided for you, Roy was no different. Father, a pipe smoking man, was very strict. He was a fit man, straight in stature, made tough by his own naval training and the tot of rum which was issued to all men as part of their ration, William Westlake drank it all his life, and sometimes when ashore, there was angry words with Ada, who would disagree that his need for rum was more important than her need for flour.

Ada Westlake cried silent tears and broke her heart as she watched her last son go off to a life in the navy at the raw age of twelve. With her life of childbearing and child raising almost over, the echoes of the songs that she sung to her small girls with their neat white pinnys would live on in the memory of Ada's children and grandchildren. Such was her story and the sands that ran through the hour glass of her life.

Family Photos (Mums side of the Family)

Westlake

MUMS STORY

Phylis, who had started life at over ten pound in weight lived the peaceful existence of childhood between wars. Food, when available, was wholesome. Porridge for breakfast or bread sops to fill your belly, it was off to school which was strict to the extreme. You only spoke when spoken too.

If school was strict, then parents were stricter. Lunch was always eaten at home, no such thing as school dinners. Meat and Veg cooked over the stove or in the oven, burnt or cooked just right, thats how you got it. Ada did not profess to be a good cook, but the menu always consisted of two choices, take it or leave it.

Four o'clock would find all the kids on the block running around in the courtyard holding a rough cut chunk of bread covered in marge or dripping, sometimes jam if pennys permitted. Father would return from foreign shores and teach his children to count in French or Spanish. He was really just a figurehead in the family and the children did not have a great deal to do with him, they just saw less of their mother when he was around. When he was there, you knew it, take the following instance.

Little Phylis excited with some news she wished to impart to her mother, entered her parents bedroom without knocking, her father was standing by the bed clothed in a vest and respectable long-jons, he turned and glared at Phylis, she ran out of the room. He put his trousers on and reached for his leather belt and came out of the bedroom shouting at her, then grabbing her with one hand he walloped her with the raw side of the belt to teach her a lesson; Not such a bad indiscretion in this day and age. Phylis never questioned her parents logic in anything.

Great Granny Norman, Ada's mother, who also lived in the flats was a formidable Victorian lady. However, she was very agile with her hands, she made Phylis a dress of tusser silk, the dress was cream and the smocking on the yolk was picked out in bright colours. Mum (Phylis) was eight years old, and the dress became her best and most prized possession, she felt like a princess, when on special days and Sundays she wore it with gloves and her new shoes. Easter and Whitsun, as poor as they seemed, there was always money for new hats, socks and white gloves to wear to church. The memory is vivid, because not long after that Phylis contracted diphtheria, she was wrapped in a red blanket for her trip to the hospital in an ambulance. When she recovered and returned home, her favourite doll and any clothes she wore were burned to destroy the germs. The lovely tusser silk dress did not fit her anymore, so Ada, her mother, gave it away to a really poor family with lots of kids. When Phylis set eyes on the dress again it was in tatters, the sight was so sad it brought her to hide away and shed tears, almost as bad as losing a dear friend.

Near the flats was a slaughter house, it was natural to see the animals herded down the street past houses and flats, most of the local men earned their living doing this work.

One night when Phylis and her sister Edna were curled up in bed, an almighty noise outside heralded the running of the cows to the slaughter house, one cow decided to split from the herd and in its confusion entered Ada Westlakes flat and found its way into the girls bedroom and in its desperate bid to escape it jammed itself between the bottom of the bed and the chest of drawers, he could go no further. The only way out was the way he came in, so William Westlake, the girls father, grabbed its tail and tussled with him whilst the girls let out high pitched screams, the cow was so frightened by all this carry on that it messed everywhere.

"Phylis, go to WICKSEYS shop and get two penneth of jam" Ada yelled, Phylis skipped off to do her bidding, it was a good sign when the budget stretched to jam. Some days when there was no money, there was no breakfast, but always a clean white starched pinny to cover your clothes, and woe betide you if you got it dirty unnecessarily. Midday they all came home and tucked into the only meal of the day. Everyone lived the same way, so you never felt under privileged. All the girls gathered in the courtyard after school to play hopscotch or skipping, but they watched the sky because as dusk fell you were expected home, so they would all disperse and disappear behind their own front doors for the night.

With no television or radio, except the crystal set that their father tapped around with at times, the fire, which was always lit would send shadows up the wall, and mother would teach the girls skills that would last them a lifetime, sewing neatly and knitting until it was time for bed. Eight boisterous and noisy children.

Sometimes a visit to Great Granny Norman was on the cards, she had been bedridden for fifteen years before she died, Mum was a tiny girl when Granny Norman, as she was to Mum, passed away, but she remembers a visit to grannys flat, standing by the foot of the bed and peering through the brass bars at the old lady propped up in bed, when a gruff voice yelled, "Get those kids out of here". They all ran for their lives.

Phylis slept with Edna and the boys, the twins, in a big double bed; Bed and board was the same thing. Fire bricks were heated near the open fire all evening and when it was time for bed, the bricks were wrapped in anything thick, like bits of old blankets, then placed at the bottom of the bed to warm your toes. The ultimate price was paid for warm tootsies, that terrible complaint of chilblains. The cure for chilblains, which was a skin irritation caused by bad blood circulation, varied from one family to another. One popular cure was to pee in the potty and stand in it, or in winter, when supplies of snow were available, it was a good cure to collect the snow in a bowl and pack your feet in the snow. Truthfully, if we examine this theory, the cold snow merely cooled the inflamed feet that burned so fiercely.

1928

Leaving school at twelve years old would horrify authorities today, but Phylis was dressed smartly and taken by Ada, her mother to BUTT, VOSPER & KNIGHT, to learn her trade as a seamstress. It was a large factory, and her sister Edna had been working there for four years when Phylis was introduced to the long working day. The factory, in Saltash Street, had the contract for naval uniforms. They also made waistcoats and top coats. Each floor of the factory had roughly two hundred and fifty employee's, some on machines and others hand sewing. Phylis started off making waistcoats, and worked her way up to being in charge of nine girls. The waistcoats had to be of the very highest standard, finished in every detail. You had to sew a demanded number a day to keep up. Wages were one penny five eighths an hour working from seven am. until five'o'clock. Overtime was needed at times to complete orders, so the girls worked through until nine pm.

The little curly haired girl, who's mother would put her hair up in rags to produce ringlets from her long blonde hair, was rapidly growing. Her favourite pastimes had always been sewing and cleaning up, she was never allowed to cook, but always asked to clean up after everyone. Even at school, the Headmaster would get Phylis to clean the office. Her pride was always in the neat sewing she produced, especially the traditional art of smocking. The highlight of her school career was the time she did the embroidered smocking on Lady Astors nightwear. It was presented to her, a woman who championed the cause of the working family, who was revered and respected by the people of the day. The award was put up in the school to announce to everyone that Phylis Lillian Westlake had been responsible for the needlework. A moment of pride to be savoured forever.

Work made little difference to home arrangements or freedom. Phylis still had to be in by nine pm. and wages given in to the household kitty, the more family members that worked the better the lifestyle. Phyl was given a precious sixpence back from her wages, she spent it all on chocolate, it was her downfall. Huge bars of Toblerone, all thick and sickly, but delicious.

Freedom Park was the favourite haunt of the young people who lived in Mount Gould. The family had by this time moved from the Buildings to Carfrae Terrace, so the park was handy. Finding a boyfriend was the ultimate reward for hours of preening and shy exchanged looks and saucy giggles. The move to this area came about when Granddad Westlake came out of the navy, he obtained work with the gas board laying all the pipes in the new housing areas, it brought in a regular income, which still stretched to the tot of rum of course.

The move to Carfrae Terrace was a good one, at last a house, with a view out over Laira, an out-lying district of Plymouth. The garden was soon full of produce, mainly potatoes, cabbage and Dahlia's. A good gardener made use of his land and William Westlake was no exception, and of course the girls were expected to help. Their role after work was to take an empty jam jar and comb the cabbage patch finding and removing caterpillars, which could consume far more cabbage than the average school kid was expected to. Phylis hated cabbage, and at mealtimes would move it about the plate, just waiting for the caterpillar that she may have missed, to appear.

One evening at Freedom Park, the gang were all there, girls and boys enjoying an 'Indian Summer' in October. "Come and meet me boyfriend Phyl, he's ever so ansome!" Nelly Fox shouted.

Nelly and Phylis had been friends, always meeting and sharing secrets in the park, so with feigned interest Phyl went to see this acquisition of Nelly Fox. Ernie Johns stood shyly, not saying a word, whilst Nelly showed him off. Phylis and Ernie's eyes met and held their gaze, just for a second, but long enough to know they would have a profound effect on each others future.

Curfew was about to arrive so they all scurried home. Phylis was tucked up in bed that night, jostling for a good spot in the bed with the rest of the crowd that she slept with. Phylis was already aware of the effects of being a young woman and the problems it brought each month, also the embarrassment of sleeping with brothers at times like this. However, sleeping with a lot of people had its compensations by being warm and comforting, and that night in October 1931 the warmth came from conjouring up pictures of the handsome young face with the piercing blue eyes. How could Nelly Fox have been so lucky!!!

Two weeks later, Nelly Fox was crying on Phylis's shoulder. "Ernie has finished with me, its all over, he's dumped me" she moaned.

"Never mind 'im, there plenty of other fish in the sea" replied Phylis lightly. It was a phrase she had heard at home many times when her elder sisters came home in tears after broken relationships. Their mothers advice was always the same "There's plenty more fish in the sea".

Phylis felt a little bad about comforting Nelly, because if the truth was out, she had accepted a date from the blue eyed Ernie. At the risk of loosing a friend Phylis continued to see him. Courting in those days consisted of long walks. They often met after work by the church at Mount Gould. Ernie lived at 5 Southern Terrace with his Mum, Dad and nine surviving brothers and sisters. Southern Terrace was near Mutley Plain, and Phylis was still living at Carfrae Terrace, Lipson Vale, so they walked through to Saint Augustus Church and up under the arch, then through to Compton Path Fields, usually the same walk because they knew how long it took. They would walk on through to Blandford Road, Efford, cut through a lane which came out at Eggbuckland Path Fields, all these areas are still there, only very populated today. The whole trip took three hours, so Ernie knew he could have Phylis home by nine o'clock.

Ernie worked for Hardings Furniture Company. It was a 'nice little earner' for Ernie, who at nineteen had tried his hand at almost everything. As an offsider to the driver of the furniture van, Ernie, would deliver furniture from the shop, then asked by the customer if he could dispose of the old stuff. Him and his mate would dispose of it alright, straight down the sale rooms it went, and they shared the proceeds of the auction.

Courting was fun, Phyl and Ern were falling in love, thats when he admitted that when he first set eyes on her, he knew she would be the girl he would marry. Phylis had never had, nor wanted to have, any other boyfriend. In December, near her birthday of the first year they went out together, Ernie took her to a haberdashery shop in Deptford Place and bought her the only present his meagre pay could afford, a box of hankies. It was to set a pattern in their lives. Even in more affluent times, Ernie would always present Phylis with a box of hankies on her birthday. Sixty years, sixty boxes of hankies, some coloured and some with lace edging, lovingly chosen and received each and every year with pride.

37 Carfrae Terrace was a comfortable home with three bedrooms, there was lino on the floor and rag rugs for every room made by Phyl's Dad, colourful rugs made with a piece of sacking for the base, the rough cut material was hooked into place and knotted individually. They were washable, durable and lasted a lifetime. When they were children, Granddad Westlake mended all their boots and shoes. He had a heavy shoe last, made of iron and when it was turned it had all the sizes on it that he needed. The kids were sent off to a shop in Cobourg Street to buy a bit of leather and nails for the purpose. Having new soles on your shoes or boots was better than cardboard, cut to fit the innersole, if it was a wet day you might just as well have gone barefoot because your socks got all soggy.

The factory where the girls worked together had a daily routine. The best part of the day was when the Claxton Siren went off. The machines and the factory would gradually go silent after a day of noise. Phylis rushed for the door with hundreds of other workers. Ernie was waiting, you see, further up the road, one day in eager anticipation she slipped and fell, twisting her ankle badly. A crowd gathered, the ambulance was called fearing a break, Out-patients confirmed only torn ligaments which meant complete rest for at least a fortnight. She spent the time lying on the settee so that Ernie could visit her every night. He worried about her very much especially when one evening, news came over the radio of two escaped prisoners from Dartmoor Prison had been spotted in the area.

The ankle healed, it was back to the grindstone. Love conquers all they say and the tongue-tied Ernie who would never say very much in front of Phyl's parents summoned up the courage when she was seventeen and he was twenty-one to ask for her hand in marriage. Phyl's family then lived at Roseberry Avenue, a lovely home in a posh part of town. Ernie stood in the polished dining room and asked her father for permission to marry his daughter. The house was situated right opposite Salisbury Road Church and Ernie looked out the window as he waited for an answer to his question. He stared at the church through the window and hoped it would either give him courage or root him to the spot. Ernie Johns was asked "What his prospects were?". His job record could hardly be said to be secure, he bounced from one job to another, even selling Marianne Margarine from a push along trolley with a bevy of fair maidens helping him at one time, but now, at the time of proposing, following a stint at labouring, he was out of work!!!

Grandad Westlake was not impressed, but then again Phylis was his fourth daughter, he had been through all this before. If Ernie only knew at the time, to win his Father-In-Law over, he should have joined the Navy, everything would have been roses.

Teaching Sunday School was another love of Phylis's, it was harmless and the children loved the doting teacher, but time spent in church was time spent away from Ernie and he resented this very much. He would wait patiently outside the church for her to finish. One night she was taking communion and it went on rather a long time, the snow had been falling gently all day, Phylis pushed open the big wooden door of the church and ventured outside. There was Ernie covered from top to toe in snow, Phyl wanted to laugh because he looked like a snowman, she thought of fetching a carrot for a nose and putting a scarf around his neck. Ernie was livid and did not see the funny side of it, he gave her an ultimatum. "Its me or the church, whats it to be?" he demanded. He liked to get his own way in all things.

During this time Phylis had contracted a bad flu virus that refused to improve, she lost weight and looked pale, and was confined to bed several times. It put a strain on their relationship because Ernie wanted to be with her and she with him. He also wanted desperately to give her a ring, to signify the fact that her father had finally given in and agreed to the engagement on the terms that they would not marry for at least two years. Money was short and Ernie although broke, was a man who stood by his principles. Phylis would have a ring by hook or by crook. They browsed around jewelry shops and agreed that the rings were too expensive for his meagre income. Undeterred they made a secret pact and went to a shop in Embrington Street. The rings there were second hand, but they picked out a pretty one, and proudly displayed it, no one ever knew it was second hand and Ernies pride was salvaged. The three stone ring cost £2.00. A full weeks wages.

Even the peace of mind of being engaged did not improve Phylis's health. Sometimes when Ernie would want his own way, she would get annoyed and one day after a jealous outburst at Freedom Park, she threw the ring back at him and ran home in tears. Early the following morning whilst getting ready for work she discovered a note had been dropped on the mat it simply read CAN I SEE YOU LATER? LOVE ERNIE X.

He got his own way again, whilst Phyl's Mum muttered "silly little fool, don't give in to him so much, or you will find yourself doing it all your life".

With her health still a great concern to both parents, her father decided to take her away to convalesce, secretly hoping no doubt that out of sight, out of mind would prevail and she might forget Ernie. Her father took her to the Isle Of Wight. Beattie and Ernie waved them off at Friary Station, she dabbed away the tears.

William Westlake enjoyed the chance to see his own Father who had a house on the island at Shanklin. It was a long two weeks for Phylis, walking along the beach collecting sea shells, she could not wait to board the paddle steamer and make the hour long journey back to Portsmouth, and the train trip that would return her back to Plymouth and the arms of Ern.

Phyls grandad, a strongman with a full beard and kindly face tried to make their stay a pleasant one. His own links with the sea were in an era before his own son, but King George VI yacht was the pride of the fleet that visited

Jenny Edwards

Cowes for the races annually. William Westlakes Father worked on the Kings yacht, lovingly tending it, involved in the arrangements that made the event one not to be missed by the yachting fraternity. Nothing could distract Phylis at all from her thoughts. She missed her love and was suffering pangs of jealousy inventing girls that the handsome and popular Ernie would be looking at whilst she was away. Ernie liked to flirt, it was part of his charm, and too most girls he was fair game. But he loved Phylis.

She need not have worried unduly, Ernie spent more time at home whilst she was away, he would send his mother out to the pictures, and then get busy moving furniture, washing floors and windows, spotless for her return. Ernies mum Sarah was a kindly woman who held her big family together by sheer guts and determination. She had produced fourteen children, nine had survived. She had lost twins when they were new born, so she had suffered her fair share of misfortune. Ernie worshipped his mother, and the feeling was mutual. One of his sisters, Doreen had damaged her leg when she was just a small toddler of two, she needed a lot of attention, and Ernie took it upon himself to see to his sisters welfare. He wheeled her about in a pram or carried her wherever she wanted to go. He often got into scrapes at school fighting battles and chasing away anyone who had teased her.

Phylis returned from the Isle Of Wight. Ernie was there at the station waiting for her to arrive. Her father, still determined not to let go too easily, put further restrictions on their romance. If the strolls they took at night went on too long, making her late home, even by one minute, she was then kept in for a week and made to scrub and clean.

Surviving all restrictions, there were happier times. Joining in events of her sisters weddings Phylis was keen to plan her own. There was Jessie, she had courted Bill Beer for about four years and they planned to emigrate to Canada, everyone was excited for them. Bill went on ahead to obtain work whilst Jessie continued to work for Mr and Mrs Kitto. She saved her money to get items for her "Bottom Drawer" which consisted of a large travelling trunk which she intended to ship out to Canada. Her sisters were given the last look at the beautiful pristine linen before the trunk was finally sealed and marked. All this took time and the letters flowed, life in Canada was good. One day, out of the blue, Jessie received a large envelope postmarked Canada, she opened it to reveal a photograph of a wedding group. There in the centre was Bill with his new Canadian bride.

Jessie broke down and cried, and went back home to her mother pouring out the whole sad story, she showed her the photograph.

Jessie held the sadness inside her and six short months later after a brief courtship, she married at the local Registry Office a man called Bert Cheeseman. He was a good choice in the eyes of her father, mainly to do with the fact that he was a naval man, he held the position of Commander at Arms. Jessie and Berts union brought forth five children, Bobby, Colin, Joy, Christine and Angela.

Jessie's broken engagement and broken heart were to stay with her forever. But thats another story.

Then there was Beattie, who gave her heart to a Musician. He played in a dance band. Jim Fitzwalter was a real 'Jack the lad' who thought he was the cats whiskers. His trumpet playing brought adulation from many girls; Being a fly by night he reveled in the attention. The band he played with travelled around and he enjoyed the adoration and sexual exploits of the girls who gave their favours. But Beattie gave her love to the handsome trumpet player who returned it only temporarily. Long enough to tie the knot at the Registry Office, which delighted Beattie who's eyes were bright with happiness. It was short lived however. Unable to conceive the children she longed for due to an accident in earlier life, she allowed herself to go under the knife to try and remedy the problem. It was a long and painful stay in hospital. Jim Fitzwalter had other plans, he took off to deepest darkest Cornwall to live with another woman who already had several children of her own. Beattie never recovered, her heart now broken, consumption set in, better known today as TB. She sadly wasted away. Phyl and Ern would visit her in Mount Gould Hospital, she was but a shadow of her former self, they scraped together precious little money they had to purchase mimosa and daffodils which were Beatties favourite flowers, but nothing could breath life into her. The sparkle appeared again in her eyes only once, when, in the dim haze of the hospital lighting, Ern would walk through the door, she said "Is that you Jim".

Wedding Photo (Mum & Dad Johns)

THE WEDDING

Now it was their turn to plan, for a start it would have to be a church wedding. Ernie insisted on it. He ran a mail order club which operated on the strangest system. The person running the club had to secure twenty customers, they each ordered something, then their names were put into a hat and drawn out. Number one received their goods with the first payment, if you were unlucky to draw number twenty, then you made twenty individual weekly payments for twenty weeks before being the proud owners of the goods you selected. Ernie made commission as well, it all helped. Phylis was making her own plans too. She wanted five bridesmaids, and a long white dress with a train, a friend at work made the wedding dress which had a fitted bodice and long sleeves. Jessie and Phyl made the skull caps that would sit on the side of the bridesmaids heads in jaunty fashion. Everyone helped with the bridesmaids attire.

Ernies Mum however, was upset when she knew they were seriously planning the wedding, she would be losing the best son a mother ever had, he was also the last son at home. Phyl had spent time visiting his home, but was always quiet and shy. Ernies sisters were stunning, beautiful, confident women who applied their makeup as if it was an art. Phyl only washed with soap and water and did not even possess a lip stick, if she had, she would not have known what to do with it! And her own father would have insisted she scrub it off anyway. Ernies Dad, who did not have much say in his own house was quite taken with Phylis, she was always polite, and never saucy towards him, as were his own daughters. He brushed passed her one day and said "Your alright maid", if that was approval, it was all she ever got.

So on August 22nd 1936, at three o'clock their vows were made before reverend Green at Charles Church in Plymouth. At the time of the marriage Phyl's parents had moved to Hewers Rowe, just off Ebrington Street, a short journey to the church. They left by taxi, it took about ten minutes, when they arrived the grassed entrance was bathed in sunlight and as they entered the church she got her first glimpse of Ernie standing at the altar beside his Bestman wearing his navy blue serge suit, crisp white shirt and blue tie. She was about to become Mrs Ernest Charles Johns.

Ernie's brother Fred made the lovely bouquet that Phyl carried, it consisted of dainty blue cornflowers surrounded by white, pink and yellow flowers of every description. Fred's economic circumstances and his love of growing flowers prompted him to offer the bouquet as a wedding gift. It was personal, as was brother Berties gift. He was a keen sportsman and won many trophys. He presented Ern and Phyl with a crystal fruit bowl edged in silver, he had won it for coming first in a race. Presents were scarce, after all it was 1936. Just the joy of being surrounded by family and friends at this time was gift enough.

The wedding ring which was lovingly chosen brand new may I add, from H. Samuels, Jewellers of Royal Parade was placed on her finger as they said "I do".

With happy smiles and laughter they all returned to the brides parents house where a wedding buffet had been prepared by her Ma. The one tier cake was cut and the decoration of flowers on top was saved. The friendly chatter with pointed cheeky wedding comments was endured by the blushing bride. Ernies brothers were a cheeky lot. Cups of tea over, married life began.

A PARTNERSHIP BEGINS

The wedding over, they boarded a tram and were waved off by Phyl's Dad. It was excitement itself to be entering a new home together. Ernie had put the finishing touches to the small flat only the day before the wedding. Phyl had never even seen it. It was at the top of fifty eight stairs, their first address together would be 11 Alexander Road, Ford, Plymouth. The family had chipped in and given them a few things to help furnish the flat. They were grateful to be starting married life with two armchairs from Phyls side and a basket chair in pink and gold from Erns Mum for the bedroom. Their bedroom suite was brand new and cost four shillings a week. The stove was out on the landing. The washing would have to be done in the courtyard at the bottom of the fifty eight steps, but who was thinking of that, when Ernie scooped her up in his arms romantically and kissed her in a way she had never known before.

They started married life with seventeen pounds between them.

THE FIRST DAY DAWNS

They awoke early with a plan to take the bouquet to the church, it was to be laid by the name plate of Jimmy Johns Jnr. who had been shot through the head in World War I. He had no choice about coming to the wedding,. He had been buried in France with his comrades in Arms. But one man who did have a choice was Ernies Dad, he did not attend the wedding, call it eccentric if you like or downright stubborn, but he said "Ern, if your Mothers going, then I won't be there".

He did not attend any of his childrens weddings for the same reason. His own marriage was not a happy one.

Meanwhile, Phylis wanted to impress Ernie with their first meal, so she purchased a piece of pork the day before. She couldn't cook, but she hoped for the best. But the best laid plans of mice and men, they say, is aft to go astray! The piece of pork was still in mothers meat safe, so off went Ernie on his bicycle, his only transport, to collect his dinner from his Mother-In-Law.

Phylis looked around her flat whilst he was gone, re-arranging little things, like the set of jugs given to them as a present. She liked the smell of the new lino, she sat trying to take it all in, she was now a married woman, and Erns rule was that if you married a woman, you kept her. So her working career was short lived, but over!!

2">

He returned shortly with the meat and stood and watched in amazement because the girl he married who seemed totally domesticated, could not cook!

Most working days after that, he would return to be greeted with a half cooked effort. He chewed his way through raw pastys and undercooked stew until his teeth could stand it no longer. He had a quiet word with his mother, who said. "Whatever you do, don't upset her, by telling her that she can't cook".

"But if I go on like this, I will waste away!" he protested. "I tell yer what, bring the maid here on Sunday for lunch, but bring her here early. She can help me cook it and pick up pointers at the same time".

"Ta Ma, you've saved me bacon" said Ernie obligingly. The plan worked and several Sundays later, Phyl could put together a reasonable roast.

Married and in love, they reinforced their feelings for one another and by the fourth month Phylis was confirmed to be pregnant. Whilst on a visit to her mothers, the naive' Phyl asked her how the baby would be born.
"It will come out, the same way it went in!" was the curt reply.

Having now completed a brief dockyard apprenticeship in Plymouth as an electrician, Ern spent hours wiring ships that were in dry dock there. When each one was completed, no one was more surprised than Ernie, when they touched the switch and it all lit up without a hitch!

He had little confidence in his own capabilities you see, but he was always a good provider.

Shortly after, a flat became vacant at 1 Caunaught Avenue, it was only two huge rooms, but it would do, even if it did have minute' fireplaces that bore no resemblance to the size of the rooms. They moved in and said goodbye to the fifty eight steps. This flat was on the first floor above the basement, however it turned out to be a cold building to live in and very soon everything they could lay their hands on went on the fire to keep them warm, including the lino which was torn up in strips and burnt. They huddled around the small fireplace with big overcoats on trying to catch the last of the precious warmth. The bedroom was even colder, one things for sure, if they had died in the night there would have been no need to take them to the morgue. The bed would have made an ideal slab.

Another move was imminent, this time to a new house. Erns favourite sister Jessie and her husband Frank rented the downstairs and Phyl and Ern rented the two rooms upstairs, they shared the kitchen and bathroom and paid twelve shillings and sixpence a week each for it. Jessie had a little baby boy called Peter, at that time. they were happy care free days at Lower Legger. The memories of card nights at Erns Mums house brought a great source of happiness. As broke as they all were, everyone emptied trouser pockets onto a wooden table in the kitchen. With a penny in the gas meter to keep the fire going, the evening was set. Win or lose, the woman would fetch the fish and chips for supper, all washed down with gallons of tea.

Then the long walk home, Jessie pushing little Peter in his pram, they passed by the vegetable fields of the Lower Compton Farm. Frank and Ern would jump the gate and pinch turnips, cabbage and potatoes, they never took more than they needed. Peters pram was used to hide the ill gotton gains, and meals for the next two days were secured.

Pamela Daisy (1st child, one year old in this pic)

MOTHERHOOD

One day in September 1937 when labour pains appeared to start, someone fetched Phylis's Mum to the house, and when Ern came home from work, not knowing what to do, he fetched his own Mother, they decided between them that it was time to escort Phyl to City Hospital. It was Tuesday, 5th September. Ernie paced up and down expecting something to happen quickly, but he was told to go home when nothing appeared to be happening.

Labour lasted three days, they knew the baby was in a breech position. Phyl was getting weaker by the hour. They took her to the delivery room in the labour ward, if this baby was to survive it would have to be manipulated into the world. It was far too late for a Ceasarean Operation. The baby was stuck in the birth canal. Getting weaker by the minute, Phylis was given an injection that sent her into a hazy half sleep, she came too after a while to see students gathered around her feet, witnessing the scene, she was too weak to protest, another injection sent her reeling, the pain was unbearable. The doctor was losing confidence at being able to save mother and child.

Ernie faced the biggest decision of his life.

"Mr Johns, its serious. I can only save either your wife or the child, the decision is yours" said the doctor.

"Do all you can to save my wife, we can have other children, but I will never have another wife" said Ernie, as he despairingly held his head in his hands.

He signed the piece of paper to take responsibility for his own actions; and waited for the outcome.

Phylis opened her eyes and looked around, she was too weak to move a muscle, she did not even know what day of the week it was. She summoned a nurse and weakly asked about the baby.

"You'll see your little girl later, when your stronger" the nurse replied.

The truth was, the six and a half pound baby girl had taken a battering during the forced arrival into the world, her little face bruised and marked badly from clamps and forceps.

Ernie was elated to know that he had a little girl, and although very weak, his wife was still with them.

Fourteen days of constant care, too frail to feed the child, Phylis found it difficult to take steps without fainting. Ernie vowed this would be their last child. I am pleased that he changed his mind or I would not be writing this now!

The little girl was christened Pamela Daisy, in a small ceremony at Charles Church. She was by then a sweet pretty baby with wispy blonde hair.

Little Peter, Jessies baby was seven months old when Pamela was born, they stayed childhood friends wherever they lived after that. Playing happily together in the back courtyard.

A whole year went by and Europe was boiling like a kettle, something was about to erupt. Neville Chamberlain, the British Prime Minister at that time, had major decisions before him. Hitler was cultivating the Hitler youth movement in Germany and the natives were restless hinting of an imminent war, no one believed it could happen again.

Plymouth had seen many wars before, it had a tumultuous history, but nothing was to compete with the terrible days ahead of the 'Blitz' that German bombers would hail down on Plymouth.

Ernie had received training in the Territorial Army, so he was one of the first to be called up when war broke out officially in 1939. Ernie, Phyl and baby Pammee had moved to Conought Road into a tenement flat, unfortunately it was riddled with mice, which was not evident when they moved in. Pammee as a toddler would crawl under the table to watch the mice crawl into a hole, she was fascinated, her mother was paranoid.

Being called up meant forced separation. Stationed off the coast of Plymouth on Drakes Island, the hard training began. The issue of Army greatcoats were not intended for the purpose that Ernie devised. The cheeky Ernie, who never missed a trick, smuggled anything he could from the island to home. If it was not nailed down, he brought it home hidden in his Great Coat when he had a leave pass.

Training over, the troops were bundled in Army Lorrys and moved up the South Coast to Bognor Regis for the final fighting techniques that would prepare them for war. The radio gave daily bulletins on the state of Europe.

Phyl missed Ernie very much, there was no leave, only letters. Pamee who missed her daddy would look out for the postman, shouting with delight when something arrived. "Daddys letter, Daddys letter" she would shout with glee even if it wasn't. She was too young to know the difference.

Before long the letters were coming from the Orkney Islands off Scotland. Gunner Johns, complete with kit bag, rifle and photo of his wife and child was by Government request stationed on the Islands. It was feared there could be an invasion off Scotland via the Islands.

The untravelled Ernie Loved the green wildness of the Orkney Islands. He was promoted to cook, feeding the troops was a full-time job, but the cookhouse was always warm. The soldiers were given their brief. They were instructed to get to know the locals and be friendly towards them to allay any fears they may have. On one of the routine foot patrols to itemise residents on the island, they came across a remote farmhouse. Several soldiers were asked into the farm kitchen to warm up with mugs of tea. The motherly lady made sure the boys had everything they needed, after all, they were going to protect them throughout the war, whatever it would bring.

The rest of the family on the farm consisted of seven daughter's who's ages ranged from fourteen upwards. They all lived there with their Mother, who ran the farm single handedly.

The farmhouse became a popular stopover on routine foot patrol, Ernie used the opportunity to light up a smoke, and write a letter home. The other soldiers, some married, some single had other ideas, and it wasn't long before clandestine meetings were arranged. The girls had never seen so many men or enjoyed so much attention, and lets face it, a man in uniform was hard to refuse especially with a war on.

During this time Ernie took a shine to Edith, she reminded him of his wife with blonde wavy hair, only hers had hints of red, her face had a few freckles which gave her a vulnerable look. Ernie promised the girls mother, that he would watch out for her, he would escort her home safely through the fields making sure no harm would come to her if she attended a camp dance. Their friendship grew. Ernie happily wrote of these events to Phylis. His vivid description of the surroundings of his island, the birds, the rugged cliffs, the pounding sea all conjoured up a pleasant picture to Phylis. It was in fact a hard existence apart from food being more plentiful than on the mainland, especially now they were friends with the farmers wife, there was fresh eggs and butter, unlike the deprivations back in Plymouth.

Ration books had been issued, food was in short supply. Phylis spent her time preparing for the inevitable shelling that took place each night. She had put together a siren suit for little Pam which was always kept next to her gas mask for convenience and quickness, there was not a lot of time to get dressed and race for the shelter when the siren went off. It had become a way of life. Who would cheat death tonight?

On the 20th March 1941, the King and Queen visited Plymouth and chatted with volunteers who worked for the war effort. Within hours of them leaving Plymouth to return to London, the deadly precision bombing began.

There had been times in the Citys history that stood out and emphasized its importance as a naval port and dockyard. It was wonderful to stand on Plymouth Hoe and watch big powerful ships glide gracefully up river and into safe harbour. Just a year before the Royal Visit, HMS EXETER limped back into dock after her gallant battle of the RIVER PLATE. The outcome was the scuttling of the German Battleship GRAF SPEE. The emotion of the Plymouth people for the hero's on board is well documented. There was cheering from the slopes of the Hoe, and it echoed around 'The Sound'. HMS EXETER had been built at Devonport Dockyard, so in effect, she was coming home. Winston Churchill, The First Lord of the Admiralty greeted her and spoke with the ships crew.

Ernest Radfords poem sums up the feeling.

Oh! What know they of harbours
Who toss not on the sea.
They tell of fairer havens,
But none so fair there be,
As Plymouth town outstretching,
her welcome arms to me.
Her breasts broad welcome spreading,
From Mewstone to Penlee.
Oh! What do they know of harbours,
Who toss not on the sea?

Poetry aside, it was the mice that finally drove Phyl out of her home, and with the help of family she moved their possessions to 87 Alexander Road, Mutley. Ernie spent some leave passes there and never wanted to go back.

Anderson Shelters were springing up everywhere, and it was in your own personal interest to locate the nearest one.

Ernie wrote to Phyl from the Islands asking her to move up there if he could arrange it, he wanted her to move into a crofters cottage that was empty, he had his eye on it for a while before writing. In his own mind at that time he visualised himself being a Farmer and provider for his family, it was never far from his thoughts. He would have been able to see his family daily, and once again share a bed with his wife. Soldiers had begun affairs with girls on the island and the farm, they made their own fun, Ern wrote to Phyl telling her about Edith, and tried to persuade her to make the decision to come to him.

Phylis was green with envy on the receipt of each letter, and regularly ended the day in tears. But she did not want to move again, fearing that he would be transferred .And she would be stuck up in Scotland, not Phylis at all.

The war which had commenced on 3rd September 1939 was now in its second year, there was no light at the end of the tunnel, daily warnings and sirens, dashing to underground shelters became the norm. Getting a pass for home leave was difficult, but not impossible. Ernies journey to Plymouth was arduous especially with the amount of kit he dragged with him, you were obliged to take everything that was issued to you everywhere. Prior to the journey he had disposed of his gas mask and filled the case with cheese, eggs, chocolate and poultry. His kit bag also contained luxurys, like food!!

His worst moment was walking along the long stone jetty to board the pilot boat to take him and others to the mainland to commence their leave, in Ernies case to commence the journey down to the Westcountry.A long Journey of over six hundred miles. His case burst open and the contraband was strewn along the rugged jetty.

"Get a move on Jono" shouted the sergeant, "Or you'll miss the bloody boat!" He turned his back as Ernie scooped up the goodies and locked them back in the case, god if that happened again, he may not be so lucky next time, he could be court-marshaled for such an offence. Ernie did not worry about minor details like that, he was going to make sure that his wife and daughter got what they needed. The Great Provider.

The joy of their reunion needed no words, there was tears as a little girl hugged her daddy, and shrieked with delight to find chocolate in his case. The meal consumed together for the first time in ages, Phylis conveyed her fears and thoughts for the future, and that night she managed to convince Ern that she would like another child. She had pleaded with him and he had given in, he would have given her anything she desired. If Phylis had been jealous and worried about the lifestyle in the Orkneys and the fear that Ernies affection was elsewhere, she needed no proof that night. They loved as never before. Pamee joined them in bed in the morning for hugs and kisses that she had also been deprived of whilst Daddy was away. She was a big girl now, all of four years old.

Transfer papers arrived, sending Ernie to Worthing, and then further on to a camp outside Bognor Regis. It was this move that seemed semi-permanent, that prompted Ernie to request his wife to come up to him, if he could find accommodation. This time she agreed, it was getting very dangerous living in Plymouth. It was to be their happiest time, if thats possible during war time with air raids, food rationing and bombing!

Phyl packed what she could for Pam and herself, there was nothing in the cupboard to worry about, so they left Plymouth on the train, following instructions she got out at Angmarin, but she had no travel documents to proceed further. Everyone had to have movement papers, in case they were stopped, you could prove why you were out of your designated area. There were very tight census rules.

51

Ernie chatted with the policeman on duty at the station, they knew each other, Ernie was familiar to him, so with a quick tongue and a bit of bribery, they furthered their journey to Rustington together. Ern took charge of the suitcase so that Phyl's hands were free, he wanted to see her face when she first set eyes on the cottage by the sea called "PAX".

The room was welcoming, the sideboard was heaving with all imaginable luxuries like sugar, tea, bread, eggs, bacon, butter and cheese. Phylis had not seen the like for several years. Each day in anticipation of their visit Ernie would discard his gas mask so he could fill the holder with food from the mess kitchen, he always managed to manipulate the stocks somehow. There was always money to be made as well, being chief cook in the mess kitchen; He had the perfect 'Deal' with the milkman who came each morning with a churn of milk, he would then take away the empty! Which was not so empty! A bob or two slipped to Ernie here and there made sure of that. After all said and done, the milkman had a wife and kids as well, didn't he?

'PAX' was a delightful single story structure facing the sea and a stretch of beach, which unfortunately could not be used as it had huge rolls of barbed wire strung across it to prevent access, as it was mined along that strip of the beach in case of an invasion off the coast. The cottage itself was surrounded by fruit trees and the front garden in pre war times would have held a riotous display of flowers. During wartime however all available ground was used to grow produce, so cabbages were flourishing in the front garden now.

The rent at 'PAX' was twelve shillings and sixpence (62 p.) and provided all the little family could desire. Mum (Phylis) memory of the lounge room is especially poignant as she recalled the fireplace with its Victorian surround, and the atmosphere of peace within its walls. Happy people had lived in that house. The world could have its war for all she cared. Many years later I made the journey to Rustington, and with the help of my dear friend Gillian who lived there, and Bob Marshall from the Air Force home on the seafront. I was able to locate "PAX" can you imagine how I felt at seeing where my parents had spent such a happy time of their War life back in 1941.

Later that day I walked along the pebble beach and thought of my mum, alive with youth, her eyes sparkled with the memoryof those days well into her 90's.

The Army Barracks was a good source of supply for Ernie Johns who brought home coal and wood. Their needs were catered for. God provided and Ernie gave him a hand!

Pam was nearly five when Phyl discovered that she was pregnant, a doctor confirmed the news, it had a great deal to do with Ernie of course and also things like the good nourishing food and tender loving care that did the trick. Their second child grew in the comfort and safety of its mothers womb. Apart from ration books and daily bulletins on the radio, life seemed peaceful in Sussex by the sea. Then Ernie was transferred again and Phyl followed to Bognor Regis. Being pregnant, Ernie decided it would be safer for Phyl to be with her own Mum back in Plymouth.

They made arrangements to travel down to Plymouth when Ernie secured a LEAVE PASS. They were living in a rented one room bedsit with use of the kitchen from the elderly lady who owned the house. They gathered their few bits and pieces together and stuffed them in a suitcase and waited for Saturday morning.

"When you off Lofty?" said the sarge.

"Not till Sat'day mornin', then I'll take me missus down to her mother in Plymouth" replied Lofty.

"I'll see what I can do, maybe get you off earlier if I can" he said.

"Loftys wife and kid need to get to Plymouth" said the sergeant to the Commanding Officer. "Can he get away earlier and catch the train tonight?"

"Can we do without him, is the cookhouse fully manned?" said the C.O.

"YES SIR" answered the sergeant as he clicked his heels together.

"Give me his leave pass, I'll alter it, bring it forward to Fridays date, but tell him from me, no mucking about, I still want him back here in ten days".

Ernie raced home, "Come on Till" he said, that was his nickname for her. "Get your things, were off now! I've wrangled it so we can go today. They boarded the train at six o'clock that night, it arrived in Salisbury at four am. the next morning with no connection for over four hours. There was nothing for it as they watched the hefty steam engine chug its way out of the station leaving clouds of billowing white smoke behind it, they would have to find the waiting room and huddle together to keep warm, wrapped around with Ernies Great Army Coat.

Dawn broke, the train arrived, which was full of troops and civilians all going somewhere that they hoped would be a safer destination. They had to stand all the way, perching little Pamee on the suitcase. The soldiers on the train were either too weary or too rude to give up their seat to a pregnant woman. Ernie put his strong arms around her comfortingly.

Disembarking at North Road Station, they caught a bus to St. Budeaux and walked the rest of the way to Phyl's Mum, who was by then well settled in her house in 3 Sunnydene. St. Budeaux. Plymouth. Her family spread far and wide, Edna, Beattie, Jessie were all married. George, Tom, Alf and Roy all at sea in some capacity, the house was now home to just William and Ada.

The leave was enjoyable. They visited Ernies Mum, and married sisters, Phyl was still shy in the company of Erns family, his sisters would swop clothing coupons, so they could dress in some of the latest two-piece costumes. Phyl always imagined she was dowdy in comparison. If the truth was known Ernie loved her for it.

All too soon it was time to part again, Ernie would have to make his way back to the barracks in Bognor. They made a pact when they parted that each night when the nine o'clock news came on the radio, with the sound of BIG BEN they would say 'I LOVE YOU' wherever they were.

On arriving back Ernie entered the mess and poured a mug of hot strong tea.

"Where the bloody hell did you spring from?" was the greeting from the troops in the mess as their mouths fell open as if they had seen a ghost!

"Where the hell do you think - I've been on bloody leave."

"Well, the house you lived in was raised to the ground on the Friday night, we all thought you was innit!!! they explained, not knowing Ernie had left earlier.

"Crikey Moses! what happened to the old dear?" said Ern.

Word got around that Lofty was alive and kicking, the beer flowed in the mess tent that night. Ernie had lots of mates and his capers and favours made him well respected. Ernie would roll a fag and have them all in stitches with a million stories.He was the life and soul of the party.

The next day he went to see the house where he had lived with Phyl until that fateful Friday night.

"What happened to the old dear who lived in this house?" he asked a neighbour as he pointed to a pile of rubble that had once been the house.

I heard she didn't want to stay in the house alone when you left for the station so she went to stay with her sister, the house was bombed that very night." he informed Ernie.

A Baby Arrives

Back in Plymouth, three weeks before her baby was due, Phyl and other pregnant mothers in and around Plymouth who were imminently expecting babies were boarded on an ambulance and taken across the river Tamar on the Saltash Ferry into Cornwall and the onward journey to Looe, an old Historic Fishing town in Cornwall, for safety. The bombing had reached a pitch in Plymouth, much of the centre had been destroyed and fires burnt for days after the shelling. Polvellen Nursing Home was their destination across the bridge in West Looe. Each day after their regular daily check- ups the women would walk across the bridge which separated East from West Looe, and down to the fish market, they sat on the seats near the Quay. The beach, although chilly at this time of year was relatively safe and the sea breezes coming around and across Banjo Pier put roses on their cheeks. Looe was a sleepy little hollow, not worth a German Bomb, thank goodness. Women were safe there. On good days there would be a gramaphone to listen to in the Church Hall at East Looe. A line of women about to give birth escaping the daily routine with the sounds of the Glen Miller Band wafting through the air.

Phyl was still interested in the news from Plymouth which seemed an eternity away.

The news was sometimes enlightening and sometimes full of sorrow. Phyl sat by the quay one day and her thoughts wandered to the year just gone and all she had endured. There was the devastating incident in Portland Square, which residents of Plymouth at that time will remember all their lives. It was the evening of April 22nd 1941, families were enjoying what for most of them would be their last meal together. At about nine-thirty that night the air raid warning had sounded. Some families made their way to their Anderson Shelter or under a steel table or maybe under the stairs for safety. But many families felt more secure in the communal shelter at Portland Square. The shelter was split up into four sections, and had escape hatches. There were bunk beds and seats. People passed the time away playing cards or having a singalong to drown the noise of heavy gunfire and the bombs. Children would scream, and they took a lot of pacifying when it was at its height. At about ten-thirty that night the area in and around the square shook just like an earthquake, and one section of the shelter filled with choking dust, it soon became apparent that the other sections of the shelter had taken a direct hit. The rescue teams were soon on the scene with many volunteers to try to dig out the dead. Out of the seventy four men, women and children who were brought to the surface only two little girls survived.

In the light of day, the young soldiers who helped to lay out the bodies showed their grief openly at the rows and rows of bodies laid out under white sheeting.

The people who lived in the vicinity were recorded, but one will never know how many people took shelter that night. Phyls friends were lost that night, Phyl had moved around because of Ernie's transfers, but most of her friends still lived in Victoria Buildings, Harwell Street, where she was born. There was old 'Lil Chapman, a good sort, and young Kenny Allen. Soldiers and the local people broke their hearts in the mortuary in Harwell Street. O'h the sadness that war inflicts.

December had arrived and the daily walks got more arduous as the birth came closer. During this time in 1942, Ernie Johns had been transferred first to Worthing and then back up to the Orkney Islands which is where he was when the baby arrived. His second child, a girl was born early on the 7th December, a much easier birth than Phylis's previous experience. A phone message to the Police Box in St. Budeaux Square sent the constable off on his bike to 3 Sunnydene. Ada Westlake (Phyl's Mum) received the news, she knew she was a granny once more.

When Ernie got the news, he wrote to Phyl and asked her to delay the news officially so he could get special compassionate leave that would run into Christmas. He desperately wanted to spend Christmas with his wife and the girls. However, his plan was scuttled, the Army checked with the Nursing Home only to discover that mother and baby were fine and there was no need for an emergency leave.

Ernie was not happy with this decision and verbally told his C.O. that if it was not granted then he would go "BLOODY AWOL!" Heated discussions followed until 'Lofty' got his own way even if it was a brief fourty eight hour pass. THE PROVIDER had won!

Whilst all this was happening Pamee was asked to name her little sister, she had no hesitation when she said Diane Margaret.

Getting to the Mainland of Scotland by boat was the easiest part of the long cold journey which involved several trains and hours spent in cold drafty carriages. Plymouth Station loomed in the distance, but the loudspeaker announced to passengers that they would have to get off the train and proceed with their journey in another manner as the train line had been blown up the other side of Plymouth. Ern lugged all his Army gear, gun, kit bag everything to the nearest bus stop and went through to Cornwall on the bus until a connection could be made with another train for the last part of the journey to Looe. Finally he made it, and as he walked the last half a mile to West Looe over the bridge, who would have known what was going through his mind.

He dropped his kit bag at the door and pushed his way through the heavy doors to find the ward where Phyl was, she collapsed in tears at the sight of him and they held each other silently. He was just absorbing the newness of his baby daughter, who had been brought in by a nurse when the Matron informed him that he only had twenty minutes left of visiting time. Following such a long journey, he was shattered and the twenty minutes became precious. He gave the nurse back the six pound four ounce bundle when the bell rang for the end of visiting. Phyl suddenly discovered that she had a temper and she felt the injustice of it all. She had waited for her husband and only been allowed the briefest of reunions. Ern had no option but to drag his bags and rifle through the cold winter wind back to wait for the train which would take him back to Plymouth to his Mother-In-Laws house so he could have a little time with his beloved five year old Pamee. Pushing tiredness aside he scooped her up in his strong arms and without thought for himself, took her into Plymouth City Centre to scour any shops that had eluded the bombing and remained open. He was determined to secure a Christmas present for her. They returned with a large wooden jigsaw puzzle. Pam loved jigsaws all her life. A few hours sleep and the long haul of getting back to Scotland began for the thirty year old Ernie. Back on the Island, the father of two returned to the cookhouse.

The events of war lead to strange bed fellows. When Ernie or 'Lofty' as he was known by everyone in the 'Mess' because he was over six foot tall, was stationed on the East Coast near Worthing. Winston Churchill checked in to one of the larger hotels in Brighton with Officers stationed with him. Plans of the invasion were being discussed and thrashed out behind closed doors. But an Army marches on its stomach, everyone knows that. The chief cook Ernie, and his many assistants were in sole charge of the catering arrangements. One night a 'Menu' for a banquet had to be prepared and cooked, there was a feeling of apprehension in the air. The word was out that important 'nobs' had made decisions which would affect the whole course of the war. Champagne was called for, indeed a night to remember, the mood was jubilant. Churchill lit his cigar and smiled confidently as he consumed the dinner and then made appropriate speeches.

Ernie and his mess house cooks relaxed in the kitchen waiting to clear up and go home. Whilst clearing up, after the party had departed, Ernie guzzled some half empty bottles of champagne, then found one that had not been opened, he hid it away until later, between him and his crew they spruced the place up, switched off lights and left. Ernie slipped the full bottle of champers inside his great coat and took it home. Next time he and Phyl would be together he would present her with it, that was the plan! There always had to be a plan....or later on in life....a change of plan!

Discharged and back to Ada's by ambulance, Phyl recovered from the birth of baby Diane. Sister Jessie, married to Bert and now with three children of her own, lived in a flat on the Sutton Trust Estate two streets away. Jessie was not coping very well, so Phyl moved in for some weeks to keep her nervous sister company, but the nightly runs to the air-raid shelters returned. A direct hit causing the deaths of an entire family in Shelly Way, threw debris in all directions. It covered the Anderson Shelter where they had taken cover. They had to dig their way out, passing children out through the hole they created with their bare hands. On returning, Jessie's home was a mess, the door had been blown in, the ceiling hung down. Furniture destroyed. Jessie had a nervous breakdown. Phyl stayed with her and supported her through it as only a sister can.

Some cheerful news arrived,they were told that if they walked to the top of Hill Park, St. Budeaux each evening, a lorry would pick up women and children and take them out to Meavy Church Hall at Yelverton on the moors. No bombing there.

They would bounce around Plymouth in the lorry collecting people from pick-up points. Soup and bread was waiting for them in the hall and they could enjoy a peaceful nights sleep on the floor. The next morning the lorry would warm up its engine and return the women to their pick-up points so they could walk the short distance to their homes if they still had one.

THE WOE OF WAR

Jessie was petrified of being alone, so Phyl stayed longer than anticipated. Barrage Balloons flew overhead, it was some help to prevent the planes from flying low, but it got so bad, there wasn't much left to bomb.

Some terrible experiences were endured without complaint. Like the time when Phyl lived in Alexander Road, Mutley. Houses all around were shelled, and on returning from the shelter one early morning she choked on the dust that filled the air only to discover a bomb had sliced all one side of a house in her street. The insides of the house were exposed like a gaping wound. A piano stood teetering three storys up. Phyl was worried about her own little home, the blast had disheveled everything. She sat and cried, tears of despair. So many near misses, was her card marked for the next time. She began to clear up the debris yet again, neighbours rallied around and helped and comforted her. They cleaned together and someone made tea. The children played, then the Mums lit a fire, the comfort from the little flame was evident. The day was coming to a close, time for blackout. Families trapped in their own time warp behind blacked out windows and streets piled high with rubble from bombed houses. The night would wake you with the sound of the droning siren warning you of a raid. With hearts pounding, families raced, sometimes five times a night, to huddle together in a shelter. A candle would be lit and put inside a plant pot and covered with another so a small glowcould break the darkness.

Servicemen would run into any shelter they could find and share it with the 'LOCALS' until the 'ALL CLEAR' was sounded. The cause one night for the siren was a German Bomber aiming to destroy the City Hospital and the Fire Station. It was tracked and followed by British Planes, in its bid to escape it discharged its total hold of bombs indiscriminately. The shells fell in line from Mutley Plain to Alexander Road. The whistling noise of the bombs filled the air and each persons heart skipped a beat until the bomb had landed and exploded ripping apart buildings and people, some whose hearts would never beat again!

The ones that were lucky, picked up the pieces and counted the dead. The casualty lists were updated and 'posted' and you had no option but to wait again for the next night to play the fateful game of Russian roulette'.

One night in a shelter they were all entertained by the beautiful voice of a negro singer, who sang soul songs as the planes roared overhead. No one knew where he came from, or where he was heading when the bombing ceased, but his music soother their soles.

It was at that time when Ernie was on a short leave pass that he saw for himself the destruction, he could not believe his own eyes; arriving by train, it shunted past his own street before coming to a halt at North Road Station. He wanted to leap from the train as he spotted, what he thought, was his own home, gutted and ravaged; He ran from the station, unaware of the weight of his kit bag, gun and everything. He fully expected the words "Sorry mate, but your missus copped it last night!"

He wanted to know, and he wanted to know urgently, more urgently than his legs would carry him. Luckily, the two room basement flat was still intact. He thought he would die himself if anything happened to Phyl. Thats when he made up his mind that she would have to be near him.

Moves were plentiful. Another base, another move, another chapter. In one house in Bognor Regis, they had rented a room from a Mrs. Hassell. Ernie heard of the room at the barracks. One Room and use of the kitchen. Ern did the gardening for the owner who was divorced from a London Solicitor, she spoke with a permanent plum in her mouth. Mrs Hassell often invited Phyl to afternoon tea and she would sit engrossed in her Devonshire accent. Pams accent had changed while they were in Sussex and she began sounding like the 'uppercrust' of England. Phyl learnt quickly that if 'ONE' spoke well to the grocer at the shop, then 'ONE' was treated like a lady!

Pam was attending school by then, a lovely little school near the sea, all flat, walking was a pleasure.

A weekend trip to the park on the edge of the water gave them an experience to remember.

Women and children played happily, it was a clear sunny day. War seemed a million miles away as Phyl leaned back leisurely on the park bench to let the sun dapple her face.

Next to her sat a lady who was resplendent in a fur coat, quite inappropriate for such a warm day, but the events that followed would prove that the coat was about to save their lives.

A noise became evident out over the water, the outline of a plane became clear, but, was it ours? was it theirs? No time to think, the rat-tat-tat of a machine gun firing bullets as the plane came almost low enough to land. The lady next to Phyl instinctively swirled her coat around herself and her child and it covered Phyl and Pamee as well. The bullets rained down, and as quick as it appeared, it was gone,. These experiences get embedded in your memory and never change or get distorted with time. The misery of war enacted day after day. Was Peace ever to come.

The planes were swallowed up in the sky. They all stayed still, fearing to move, for what seemed like forever. Shaking all over, they checked the children. They were safe, thank God, apart from scratches and grazing from quick movement when they fell to the ground. The two women were fine, but the coat was riddled with a line of bullets caught in the swirl of the hemline as the coat swung out and around to envelope them. Phylis had to agree, that if she had been a cat, she was rapidly disposing of her nine lives.

WINNIES CHAMPAGNE

Ern finished his long shift feeding, cooking and cleaning for the troops in the cook house. He was eager to get home as he skipped along the cinder path beside the tennis court, he turned the corner and went inside, "Hi, Till'" he said as he planted a kiss on her cheek. He took of his coat and then rummaged around and got out the champagne he had been saving.

"Look what I got er' Till" He said.

"Whats that?" She replied.

"I got one of Churchills bottles of champagne, I kept this one for you" He said.

"You devil! You shouldn't have done that, one of these days you'll get caught" She exclaimed in disgust.

"So what!" Said the daredevil Ernie. "Drink up and pretend we are somewhere else."

Phylis was not impressed with the taste equating it to lemonade with extra bubbles!! But it worked and spruced up their love life that night, and made her temporarily forget the bad experience of the day.

Once again, the provider had done the business .In that memory, Dad always said that's where Diane came from?

Ern insisted that Phyl did not go to the park again when he heard what had happened, but there weren't many places for young children to play. The bombing had increased on the East Coast. The land was flat, no hills for cover. The planes would do a silent run in and they weren't detected, then out of the blue the bullets rained down on you.

Ernie was by then having regular medical check-ups on his ears which were often bursting when he was operational on the big guns.

LOAD   STAND CLEAR   FIRE!!!
LOAD   STAND CLEAR   FIRE!!!
LOAD   STAND CLEAR   FIRE!!!

He suffered badly from shattered ear drums which would leave him in pain. The sort of pain that did not subside with a few pints of beer in the 'MESS'.

The Army finally discharged him and returned him and his family back to Plymouth in 1944. Pamee was seven and Diane two. Jobs and accommodation were few and far between, so they moved in temporarily with Edna, Phyl's elder sister. She was now married with three children, Terry, Shirley and Gerald. The house had three bedrooms, but with four adults and five children, it was well and truly over crowded and noisy.

Mrs Hassell, who's house they had lived in until he was discharged from the Army started writing to Ernie, mistaking all the friendship he had shown for overtures of a different kind. In one letter she openly invited the handsome Ernie to leave his wife and come and live with her. She assured him that he would want for nothing! All Ernie wanted was some peace and quiet, so he tore the letter up and never replied.

Ernie tramped the streets by day looking for rooms to rent for his family and a job to pay for the rent.

He knocked sheepishly on the door of a house in 18 Oxford Avenue, Mutley. Someone had given him a tip that there was an empty room. Minnie Harris, the only other occupant agreed, in the absence of the landlady to let the three vacant rooms upstairs to Ernie. She felt sure it would be alright as long as Ernie's wife took it in turns to clean the flight of stairs. The job he later secured in the Dockyard as an Electrical Fitter would provide the rent money.

They settled into their new abode and enjoyed six months of quiet domestic bliss, the war had changed its course and more and more of it was fought in Europe. Tactics were forcing the enemy to retreat. Minnie enjoyed the company of the little family; She worked in the Plymouth Market in Old Town Street on a vegetable stall and Phyl got into the habit of lighting her little fire and putting the kettle on low just before she was due home. In return she would sometimes babysit so Phyl and Ernie they could go to the pictures at the BELGRAVE CINEMA off Mutley Plain.

Mrs Smith, the landlady owner of the house who had been in Wales for six months returned unexpectedly. She was most annoyed that the flat had been let. She was a wizened old witch of a person and they later discovered that her poor husband had committed suicide by decapitating himself with a Japanese sword in the very room Ern and Phyl used for their bedroom.

Things calmed down a bit and Ernie offered to decorate the rooms to spruce up the house, he had done this kind of work for years before the war to earn extra money. He was good at it. Mrs Smith offered to pay half towards the cost, she was mellowing. She waited till it was completed and when Ernie called her up to take a look she said it was fine but denied offering to pay half. There was hell to play, Ernie was spent out on the project, but apart from throwing the old witch down the stairs he could do little or nothing about it.

Discharged from the Army, Ernie was learning to cope with civilian life once more, but it was comforting to live and work close to all their family once more, without fear of being transferred, they went to Ernies Mums every Sunday for lunch, and Phyl was able to see more of Ada, her own Mum who enjoyed the company of her two grand-daughters who were growing away. Little Diana had a determination not usually seen in a child so young. Ernie had made her a little push along horse with a handle she could lean on, it helped give her confidence to walk, which she did unaided at the tender age of ten months. To keep her quiet because of the stroppy landlady, Phyl spoiled her, anything she wanted, she had, there could be no tears or temper tantrums in case they would be in trouble with 'ER DOWNSTAIRS!!

Whilst living in the flat at 18 Oxford Avenue, the arrangements for having a bath were the same as everyone else at that time. The wash house had a big copper boiler, you lit a fire under it with anything you could get your hands on, old shoe boxes, sticks, a little coal if you had any, as long as you could keep it burning until the water got hot. The old tin bath was hung on the wall when not in use. When you needed a bath, you locked yourself away in the wash house and poured hot water from the copper into the bath and then got buckets of cold water from the taps outside in the yard to cool it down.

Erien was planning to go to his Saturday Football Match at Argyll, when he was organizing his bath. Everything was ready and the water just right, so he stripped off and got in for a good soak. The sunlight was breaking through the slats in the old wooden door, all of a sudden he couldn't see the sun, only shadows. Then it dawned on him that someone was looking in, it was the old witch of a landlady peering through the crack to get a gander at his manhood! He moved slowly reaching for an old jug, he filled it with bath water and without warning he aimed it at the door. She let out a shriek, howling her head off. Ernie called her a "Dirty old bugger!" But he got the better of her.

THE LOSS

It was a sad year in many ways. The sands of time ran out for Ada and she passed away at the young age of fifty eight. She suffered a cerebral Haemorrage on the 12th March, 1944. The tears flowed as they gathered to bury Ada at Weston Mill Cemetery. The pain of the loss was obvious, Phyl was fortunate in having the support of Ernie to help her through it. But just one short month later, whilst calling around to visit his parents Ernie found his Father collapsed, it was discovered later that he had suffered a stroke, he died the same day on the 12th April 1944. Phyl and Ern were in deep shock. The loss of two parents so close together.

The grief of these losses put a cloud over their lives, but they had two little girls, who had also suffered the loss of two loved grand-parents so quickly. Ernie's Mum needed Ernie and he split his time between Phyl and Sarah (his mother), always kind, always supportive. He took the role of provider for both families.

Summer came and went. The war in Europe still raged.

Christmas was planned and enjoyed. Ernie would plan little treats. For sixpence he would take his small daughters into Spooners Christmas Grotto, it was a magical fairyland. What pleased him, would delight his children. He went up to Central Park, one late night before Christmas and dug up a fir tree, he brought it home and they decorated it with coloured paper and streamers. Pamee and Diane would shriek with delight. Small gifts of french knitting sets, skipping ropes and bright ribbons would be left under the tree to please their happy little faces in the morning. But always after Christmas by the 29th December, he would have purchased the box of hankies for Phylis for her birthday. By 1944 she already had eight boxes. The first box of hankies cost Ernie one shilling and eleven pence, three farthings.

They owned a big leather poufee' it had a zip underneath and made a perfect seat for a small child. This was Phyl's hiding place for all Ernies letters whilst he was serving away. She would read them, savour each loving word and file them away in the poufee'.

END OF THE WAR IS NIGH

Nature has no regard for war. In Springtime the flowers fought their own battle for survival and supremacy to open up in the sunlight. The beautiful Beech tree unfolded its delicate pale green leaves until by summer the boughs were heavy and full. The sun shone brightly, mothers picked primroses with their daughters. Clothes were scrubbed and patched a hundred times before being discarded.

Plymouths Pier which had enjoyed the company of Edwardian ladies sauntering on its structure when it was built in 1884. Was 'BLITZED' in 1941. Until then it was a distinctive landmark with its Domes, wrought iron railings and prominent clock face. Dances were popular and so were the summer shows and afternoon teas. 'Regatta Day' was one of the most eagerly awaited social events on the Calendar. Crowds congregated on the slopes of the Hoe, to watch the racing. The 'BLITZ' was also responsible for partially destroying Charles Church where Phyl and Ern were married. The powers that be kept the ruins, even to this day. Not as Ernie always said because they had married there but as a stark reminder, not only of the 'BLITZ' but also of the 'CIVIL WAR'.

During the final year of the war, the City of Plymouth had suffered 59 raids of various strength. Nearly 5,500 casualties were recorded, about 1,900 of which were fatal. Over 4,000 houses and business premises were totally destroyed or damaged so extensively that they had to be demolished. A further 18,000 homes were seriously damaged. But victory was now in sight.

The second world war was the greatest test for the British nation in its entire history.

The prospect of forced separations had quickened the pace of courtships, and the war years saw an upsurge in marriages. Many British girls fell for foreign servicemen, particularly continental charmers, so exciting compared with the reserved conduct of their own countrymen.Lots of girls sailed off to America following brief romances with service personel.

After the Allied Breakout and sweeping advances in France during the summer of 1944 there was some relaxation of Blackout regulations, with subdued lighting being allowed at busy road junctions. Many of the Home Guard forecast Germanys demise before the end of the year. But this was not to be.

By the Spring of 1945, peace, at last, seemed just around the corner. The R.A.F. and U.S. Bombers continued their massive aerial bombardment of German targets. The Third Reich reeled and by late April, the British based bombers set out no more. Everyone expected some last minute revenge tactics. But news came that HITLER was dead, and May 8th, 1945 was officially proclaimed as Victory in Europe Day - VE DAY. There were street parties everywhere, bonfires were lit and improvised fireworks let off to celebrate the event.

But it was not all over, there was still Japan to defeat and troopships still sailed out of Liverpool, bound for the Far East. Japans defeat was only a matter of time.

The Labour Party won a landslide victory in the June elections that year, which saw the disbandment of Churchill's National Coalition Government. Clement Attlee replaced Churchill as Prime Minister.

The dropping of two atomic bombs hastened Japans defeat and they surrendered on the 14th August 1945. The next day Britain celebrated the war's end, Victory over Japan. VJ-DAY.

PART TWO

PART TWO

A FAMILY AT PEACE

Peace was now established and Phyl was enjoying life again with Ernie. They had hoped for a son, when, with the war over, they planned to increase their family. Ern was disappointed when at 6.30 am. on the second of October, he was blessed with another daughter who was born at 18, Oxford Avenue. Jennifer Mary weighed in at 6lb. 4ozs. She was quickly wrapped in a shawl and placed in a wicker laundry basket where she slept contentedly. The basket fitted neatly under the table where the wireless sat. When it was on and blared out music the baby girl slept. When the radio was switched off, she woke and cried. Jennys love of music obviously started from birth.

It was a good job Jenny was a quiet baby, because the witch of a landlady never gave Phyl a moments peace. If the pram was left in the hallway after a trip to the shops, it would be flung up the stairs without ceremony! Mrs Smith hated children, and she had no intention of tolerating Phyl and Ernies growing brood. One Friday night Minnie Harris had offered to babysit so they could enjoy a visit to the pictures, all was well until they were walking down the road and came face to face with the Landlady and her daughter and son-in-law who was built like a brick chicken house!

"I suppose your here to sort me out" said Ernie.

"Thats the general idea" replied the man.

They disappeared up a side alley, leaving the woman to wait for their return. The noise of punch upon punch was heard and Phylis feared for Ernie. He came out of the alley straightened his tie and as he walked off wiping the blood from his face, he said to Phyl "Well, we won't hear anything more from them!" They decided that another home would have to be located if they were to have any peace at all.

In the next six years the family grew to five children. One of Ernie's proudest moments came when his sister-in-law Edna, who had looked after Phyl throughout this birth, announced that Phyl had given birth to the son he longed for. Brian David Charles Johns had broken the mould on the 29th January 1949. He was a happy healthy baby who was quickly nick-named 'Lardy Head' because he had no hair on his head until he was at least six months old.

GOODBYE SARAH

The happiness of having a son was short lived. Baby Brian was one month old when Sarah, Ernies Mum who had been a widow for five years since the death of his father, was admitted to Hospital. She had to have an operation to relieve a huge build up of fluid, the actual operation seemed successful, but a blood clot took her life before she recovered, she was seventy-one years old. Ernie cried for days, he was devastated. Apart from Phylis, his mother was the only other woman he truly loved. Coping with her death was a daily battle, tears would fall without warning. Sister Daisy went to their mothers home to sort things out and discovered thirty five pounds hidden under her mattress with a note asking that it be used to bury her.

Edith, the eldest daughter claimed the most valuable possessions and Ernie was asked if he wanted anything as a memento of his Mum. He went to her house but he needed nothing to remind him of the strong fearless woman that he had adored all his life. She had given him his values, his humour, and above all she had given him her song. Her strengths had surpassed all his imagining and now she was no more. He left the house carrying two blue china figurines. He closed the door behind him, it made a hollow sound as he walked into the street. A mist of tears blinded his eyes. He returned home and lifted his son from the pram and held him so close that Phyl feared he would crush the small baby, but she understood. No words were needed.

Ernie buried his mother in the same grave as his father, he scattered the earth over her coffin as he said his silent goodbyes, and went on to the next chapter in his own life. HE was thirty seven.

They had recently moved to a top floor flat in Kathleaven Street, it was a large airy flat owned by the Sutton Trust. Pam and Diane were enrolled at Victoria Road Primary School. Three year old Jenny would perch up on the sofa and look out of the window, eager for their return. Phyl's girls all had long hair, blonde haired Jenny would submit to endless hours of hair brushing and individual curling of every ringlet. When she was just four years old, Pam took Jenny to the dancing class at Victoria Road. Pam was twelve by then and very motherly towards her two younger sisters. She had heard they were auditioning for a small child to sing 'ME AND MY TEDDY BEAR' Jenny learnt the words and stole the show. A born actress!

Next door to Grandad Westlake in Sunydene a house had become vacant at number five. Phyl played on the fact that she needed to be near her widowed father to care for him. It worked and they were allocated the house. Moving day saw lots of breakages by eager hands. Pam and Jenny walked on down to the new house carrying a small tin bath with bits and pieces in it, and they waited in the garden for the removal van to arrive.

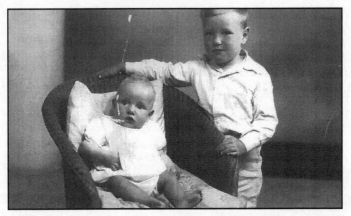

Derek 6 months & Brian Johns 3 yrs

THE FINAL MOUTH

Settling in at 5 Sunnydene was no hardship, it was a bright house with garden back and front. Ern and Phyl were careful with their money, the bills were all paid on time. Weekly picnics at Plym Bridge were enjoyed. With extra painting and decorating, there was always money to buy new clothes for the children at Whitsun and Easter. They were content with their lot.

One night, Phyl broke the news gently to Ern that their fail-safe method of contraception had failed, she was pregnant at thirty-six. The idea grew on them and they both got used to the 'surprise baby'. On January 26th 1952, a seven pound boy was born to Phylis in the front room of 5 Sunnydene. The rest of the family were asleep upstairs during the birth. When they awoke, Ern hoisted one on his shoulder and scooped the other two under each arm, and with Pam at his heels they descended the stairs to take the first peek at their new brother lying in the bed next to their Mummy.

Derek Raymond Keith Johns was christened in the same church as his brother Brian, in a small service at St. Boniface Church where the blossom from the trees surrounding the building had fallen to make a pink carpet.

The family was close knit, bonded by the very roots of the generations that preceded them. In 1952 the country suffered the loss of their beloved King George. He passed peacefully away and whilst the Queen grieved, her young daughter, The Princess Elizabeth was flown home from an overseas visit with her husband to plan for her own Coronation.

Street parties were organised for Coronation Day. June was a glorious month, the sun shone brighter than ever before and England had a new young Queen.

Cups were presented to all children amidst the celebrations. The red, white and blue bunting waved enthusiastically as crowds cheered "LONG LIVE THE QUEEN".

Every year Ernie would decorate his home with new wallpaper and paint. There was always the ritual of trimming the edges of the paper before the pasting could begin. This time he planned to wallpaper the ceiling with paper that had stars on it, Jenny had chosen it. The paper was trimmed and pasted on his paste table, then with a plank of wood balanced on ladders he commenced to paper the ceiling. All the children laid on the floor looking up to admire his handiwork. Ernie hated it, it looked just like he had removed the roof and we were all under the stars! It had to go, so the next day, on went the emulsion and goodbye stars.

He worked long and hard to rear the little family; They all had his traits, some more than others and he loved that. Brian was always bartering to secure a 'DEAL' or a good 'swop' even if he got the worst end of a DEAL! Derek was a shy child, who hated the rain, but he could always get around his mother to have first pick of the 'fancies' at the Sunday tea table.

Each Sunday throughout the summer months would see them pack a suitcase of goodies and with the children dressed in Sunday best, the family headed for the countryside at Plym Valley near Marsh Mills. It took two buses to get there, and then a mile walking to the family 'SPOT' where all the sand shoes and camp fire equipment had been hidden in the bushes to save taking it home each week.

The childrens clothes were changed for play gear and hung neatly on nails hammered into a tree for the purpose. A fire was lit, and children scampered off in all directions to fetch cool clear water from the waterfall and sticks to keep the fire going. Dad would make camp tea, and boil spuds over the open fire, and us kids would create adventures of our own in the Jungles of Plym Bridge! After a full day of playing cricket and mucking about in the river was enjoyed, everyone was suitably worn out. Sometimes Aunty Jess and Uncle Frank, Aunty Daisy and Uncle Ken, and all their offsprings, plus numerous other relatives with children would join us. At the end of the day, washed and dressed again in Sunday best the whole family would trek along the disused railway line back to civilization and the two buses which would take them home.

A Johnsy Christmas

Christmas was the best time. Shopping and preparing until the event occurred. Ernie was the provider, and always looked up to. After all there was nothing he couldn't get or do.

The kids would be treated to a visit to Santas Grotto, it was all part of the ritual even though some of them were convinced that Ernie Johns had a second job at Christmas Time, as Santas right hand man! Leading up to the festive season, it was customary to let the kids write a letter to Father Christmas. The mantelshelf with the gentle tick of the clock, flanked by the precious blue figurines over looked this annual event, as did the two love birds painted on the mantle mirror.

The notes were written and folded then with Ernies (Dads) guiding hand at the right moment they were aimed up the chimney, the upsurge would fly them to the top where theoretically Father Christmas would read the note. If it came back down again and burnt up on the coals, then you had to write it again or there would be no knowing what you might end up with on Christmas morning!

Weeks in advance Diane and Jenny would search all the wardrobes and cupboards seeking out stored gifts, and upon discovery, they would decide who they were for. They were seldom right, but what did it matter. The thrill of looking was suitably satisfied. Christmas Eve held the other ritual of choosing one of Dads socks, to hang up, preferably, not one with a hole. It was a festive highlight, and on Christmas morning they would discover what their stocking held, one orange, one apple, a handful of nuts and some toffees, how sweet the memory.

The day would commence with Ernie eating a more than hearty breakfast, whilst the brood sat around the tinseled tree examining the gifts beneath it. They waited patiently for what seemed like an eternity. Eventually, with undivided attention, the giving out of presents began, with each one receiving the same amount. When that was over, each would find a corner to study the gifts more closely. If it happened to be a post office set it was all set up, or the girls favourite was always a miniature cooker with a set of saucepans to match. They would light a candle and put it inside the little cooker, then use the saucepans to create the real thing, like chips or porridge!

The 'CROW SHOOT' was a favourite for the boys. Bows and arrows or bikes, which were generally absent a few bits and pieces by February. Then Ernie would commence the 'WORK AND SAVE' routine all over again with Phyls constant support.

The house at this stage was often bulging at the seams with pets, generally the sort that "followed" Jenny home. There was Spot the dog, Whisky the cat, Bluey the budgie, a couple of white rabbits and a hamster or two. On top of this menagerie, Ernie kept a chicken house, which provided enough eggs to feed everyone and the chickens disposed of the household food scraps. Have you ever smelt potatoe skins being boiled and cooled to feed chickens, the smell remains in your nostrils forever.

When the family fell on hard times, the chicken run was depleted, they were killed off and eaten one by one until finally the only one left was 'MATILDA'. We would rather have starved than eat 'MATILDA'. But food was scarce, so Matilda was for it! Ernie cornered her in the shed with the broom handle, and using the small axe he cut her head off and left her hanging upside down to drain! The kids were all sitting on the back door step when he emerged. That day they all learned that their Father was human too. Dinner was dished out and there was 'MATILDA' cut into chunks floating on the plate with vegetables and gravy. No one spoke, and suddenly everyones appetite disappeared. What a waste, and what a dirty murderer Dad turned out to be!!!

GETTING BACK IN
THE GOOD BOOKS

Ernie tried to make up for disposing of beloved Matilda by building a little play house in the garden for the girls, it was complete with window boxes full of flowers, and there was a swing built of wood and rope. Ernie was clever with his hands and a bit of wood and some six inch nails! He was also a good gardener, and grew produce readily, whilst next door Granddad Westlake grew fruit. Gooseberries flourished, and Derek learnt at a very early age which ones to pick. There was also blackberries which were picked until the juice ran down your fingers and stained your hands. Lovely days.

School Holidays would see Diane and Jenny with the dolls pram, going to Victoria Road Primary School to claim their free milk, then they would join the queue again until the lady recognised little angelic faces and said "Not you two again". With all the little bottles of milk stashed neatly behind dollys pillow, they left the playground with big grins on their faces. Daddys traits, you see!!

Diane and Jenny had spent an entire childhood with Miss Tolleys Dancing Troupe'. There were shows to rehearse for and costumes to make. Phyl was good in this respect with her background in needlecraft. She could whip up flower costumes made from green and blue satin or sailor suits. The memory of the 'BUBBLE' dresses for the sequence of "I'm forever blowing bubbles" is so tangible, they were wonderful with huge puffs of celephane.

Every Friday night and generally speaking, Sunday Lunchtimes as well Ernie went to the pub for a pint, sometimes with his Father-In-Law William Westlake. Their 'LOCAL' was the Trelawney in St. Budeaux. Phyl could never get the kids asleep until they heard his key in the door.

"Dad, have you got any crisps" they enquired.

He would jump the stairs two at a time, push open the bedroom door and drop the packets on the bed, there would be an almighty scramble. Just the thrill of finding the blue bag of salt would keep them awake. Jenny would swop crisps for the salt bags and eat it like sugar.

Sunday lunchtime the drinking duo would come home merry.

"Is my lunch in the kitchen" enquired granddad Westlake.

"Yes, on the table" replied Phyl. She always cooked extra for her Dad.

No one ever told him that later it was discovered that he had eaten what had been left for the cat! Complete with cat food mixed in!!!Theres more to Kit-e-Kat than meets the eye.!!

Sunday afternoons the family were sent off in their Sunday best to Sunday School, with a penny for the collection plate, which was usually spent at the corner sweet shop. Mum and Dad would go to bed for a well earned rest, or thats what we were told anyway!

Brian and Derek were catching the girls up fast in years, and were as devilish as any boys their age, and the joy of getting away without paying your fare on the Saltash Ferry by hiding in the toilets was great until it wore thin the day the ferry was stranded midstream for one and a half hours. Two pence was not a fortune after all.

Another day they decided to swim to the boats anchored half way across the River Tamar, beneath the towering shadow of the Brunel Bridge. They quickly tired of this pastime however and wanted something a bit more adventurous, so they decided to swim all the way to the Cornwall side, but just after they set off an undercurrent had risen and it sucked them downstream and as it swirled around the pillars that supported the bridge, they thought they were goners! Gulping water and gasping for breath they were washed up on the "Salt Flats" exhausted.

"Don't tell mum" said Brian, "She'll kill us!"

They stuck to the safer pursuit of crabbing after that.

Pocket money was given out weekly so the kids could go to Saturday morning pictures. Sixpence for the movie show, which would be three hours long. There was generally a cartoon, then a Laurel and Hardy sketch, and to finish off, Buffaloe Bill would do his stuff. Three pence would buy an everlasting strip, some sherbit dabs, refreshers or spangles! Enough to last a kid through a three hour picture show.

Pamela, an average scholar, enjoyed looking after her brothers and sisters, she had been a second mother to Derek from the moment he was born, but she was now old enough to go out to work. Spooners, the Department Store, had a vacancy for a junior. Phylis took Pam along, just like Ada had taken Phyl to her first job all those years ago. Pam was very shy, but she got the job working in the hardware section. The small weekly wage she happily spent on her brothers and sisters, taking them to the matinee at the Cinema after work. They would wait for her with bread and jam sandwiches in a paper bag. She would always buy an icecream tub at the interval, or an orangemaid, which was made from real oranges. What a loving sister she was.

THE HOLIDAY

One year, great excitement prevailed. There had been talk of a caravan holiday. Ernie's boss had let him have it cheap by way of repayment for a job well done. The caravan was at Challaborough, up the Devon coast. Ernies boss picked them all up in his car and took them to the site near the beach. O'h the view from the hill across to Burgh Island as they walked around the cliff top and down the lane. Everyone was settled in and getting used to the new experience of trying out the bunk beds when Ernie walked back up to Bigbury to wait for Pam at the coach park. She could not start her holidays until she finished work that evening.

Each day held a new excitement. Ernie and Phyl set up little races for the kids, Ernie would time them to see who could run to the general store and back in the quickest time. Just a bag of sugar or bottle of milk, only one item per run was required, but they all had a go. Heart pounding coming back up to the caravan; it was all so important, it moulded a competitive spirit, which was always needed anyway when they grouped around a table to play cards, much to Phyls disgust, they were all good at cards, not just the average childish games of FISH or SWITCH! All of Ernies kids could play BRAG or POKER, but there was always a wager on the side. Ernie was a true gambler, and would bet sixpence on two flys climbing up the wall. The kids thought the world of their

Dad and often vied with Phylis for his affection, but he was big on love, there was plenty to go around. Saturdays was horse racing day. Ernie would scribble his bets on a piece of paper, fold it and put his money inside, hand it to Jenny or Brian, to "Take it to Yorkie" he was the local SP bookie? If you were asked to go there…you gave Yorkie the bet and scarpered. The house smelled of old frying oil.

The years rolled on and in 1956 Phyl and Ern celebrated their Twentieth Wedding Anniversary. A family of three daughters and two sons, who could ask for anything more.

Pam had been working for a number of years, transferring to the Co-op from Spooners, when it was time for Diane to start work.

Diane secured a good job with a family firm called CHURCHILLS, the shop was in Westwell Street and it sold Fish, they were also the Purveyers of high class game, Pheasants hung outside the shop and it was popular with the Landed Gentry. Dianes position was cashier, she was good with figures and had a ready smile. She had a couple of boyfriends but no one of any consequence. Phyl and Ern had been spectators as they watched both Jenny and Diane fall for a handsome boy called Raymond Walters, who joined the Merchant Navy and sent romantic letters to both of them. However, Diane being three years senior to Jenny had first claim. The presents sent from foreign shores was an obvious draw card, and Raymonds shore leave was spent in Plymouth mainly with Diane. Jenny tagged along when she was allowed to.

With Pam now working for the Coop and Diane employed by Churchills, they were in a position to purchase nice clothes. Jenny borrowed most of it before she turned fifteen, much to the disgust of her sisters. Phyl and Ern would step in and calm the fighting trio. Their fights were short lived however, there wasn't anything they would not have done for each other. They all slept in the same room, so it was important to get on.

Brothers were a different kettle of fish, they were fine to play wagon trains with on the bed when they were younger, but they were a real pain when the courting began.

Especially Brian, who had an 'A' for pest! He worked hard at annoying the hell out of his sisters and it sure was difficult to impress a new boyfriend when your eleven year old brother made snorty noises, and then wiped his nose on the sleeve of his jumper. Brian had it all sorted out! His theory was that if the boys returned after this treatment, they were worth furthering, if they did not, well, they were just cissys anyway. Brian faced all the missiles of life with cheerful defiance.

Phylis and Ernie Johns held the family together with love, it was boundless, and there was always plenty of reserves. It proved to be far more precious than money in the bank as the future took shape. Ernie now had a full-time job with Plymouth Cooperation, painting and decorating. His brother Bertie, who had moved to Cornwall after a family upset regarding the paternity of one of his children, would sometimes do a contract with him for private work, decorating or sign-writing, no job was too big or small, they tackled anything.

When the situation demanded it, Ernie worked away for a while, up in Exeter. He always came home at weekends, but Phyl had not endured this type of separation since the war and she hated it. The landlady at his 'Digs' gave him the old 'come-on' look and back to Plymouth he came with his tail between his legs. Ernie had plenty of bravado where the ladies were concerned, as long as they didn't try to get on top of the situation, if you know what I mean. Then his fast tongue would turn into fast legs so he could retreat rapidly!

A THIRD WORKING DAUGHTER

It was now almost time for the third daughter, Jenny, to go out to work. She was a worry, this one. Artistic, dramatic, with stars in her eyes she put in an application to join the circus at the age of thirteen, to work with the elephants!. Phyl and Ern knew nothing about it until BERTRAM MILLS CIRCUS, unaware of Jennys age, wrote inviting her to come to their winter quarters in Manchester for an interview.! Jenny was as unpredictable as the weather, she had a rare zest for life and all it could offer, and saw no danger in anything. Phyl's hair showed signs of greying, keeping up with this one. Where her future lay, no one could tell. She adored children and animals and was good with both, so they hoped she would obtain work with either. HILLAWAY HOUSE CHILDRENS HOME in Tavistock offered her a job, but it would mean living away from home. Ernie wouldn't hear of it, his family would stay together until he decided otherwise. Undeterred, Jenny secured her own employment, close to home, to keep Dad happy.

Where do the lines begin to be traced that lead two people together in this life? How far back lies the origin of their destinies? Whatever the answer, romance blossomed for Pamela who was tired of everyone thinking she was courting the fireplace! Jimmy Simpson, her first love became just a memory when she met Gerald Baker at a family wedding. He had dark continental looks and rode a BSA motorbike. He spent some time ingratiating himself with Ern, he even offered to teach him to drive a motor car! The purchase of the Hillman, complete with running boards was a moment of triumph for Ernie, even if it spent more hours parked outside the gate than actually on the road! Diane was seriously courting a young man named Michael, who was also an owner of a motor car, they exchanged motoring language, Michael was more interested in what went on under the bonnet whilst Ernie could only envisage painting the body work with thick grey cooperation paint.

The proud moment arrived, Ernies couple of driving lessons out on Yelverton Air Strip going backwards and forwards in the same manner as a kangaroo hops over the Australian Desert was enough to give him the confidence to arrange a Sunday drive out across the Moors! With Ernie at the helm, the Hillman hopped its way through roads that dwindled into country lanes. The gears grated regularly, the horn was honked...mainly by other drivers! The picnic spot was in sight, with an excited yell from the kids in the back, the fan belt politely split in two, to show Ernie what it thought of his driving skills.

Stranded on a Sunday afternoon out on the Moors was not a problem, there was a picnic and varying suggestions from accompanying relatives on how to rectify the problem to enable them to get home. This driving lark was not the piece of cake Ernie hoped it would be and he felt strangely inadequate.

The age of the motor car soon passed for Ernie, and after footing the bill for repairs, and painting the thing with Michael's assistance, Ernie got very little use from it. Pams Fiancee' Gerald offered to keep the engine ticking over, and regularly used the thing. Jenny and her boyfriend Leslie (Eddie Edwards)also took it for a spin a few times. Les drove for a living, and it annoyed Ernie that younger men could do something that he had no knack for! The car would have to go. With not a word, he advertised the sale of the Hillman, and as the advert goes, THE FIRST TO SEE-WILL BUY! Thats just how it was.

Pamela's Wedding

Pamela married Gerald Baker in March 1960. Diane and Jenny were part of a group of five bridesmaids, Pam had wanted the same things as her own mother had, all those years ago. Erns speech held humour and pathos, and with great reluctance he and Phyl watched the first one leave the nest.

The honeymoon over, Pam settled down in a ground floor flat in 28 Oxford Avenue, Mutley to commence her married life. The flat was just a few houses away from where Phyl and Ern had lived towards the end of the second world war. As a doting Father, Ern papered and painted the little flat and provided little things to start his Pamee out on her married life.

If Pam had thought she was marrying a duplicate of her father, she was very quickly disillusioned. She visited Sunnydene often and never complained of a marriage that was far from happy, she was a homely girl who enjoyed the closeness of Mum and Dad, and she was finding it hard to adjust. When she discovered she was pregnant, they were the first to know. She carried her baby well and spent most days down with her Mum, she was cheerful as the springtime birth drew closer. Pam was an attractive young woman with thick dark hair, like most women before her, she blossomed with pregnancy.

That night after Pam returned home, Phyl and Ern sat together on the settee in front of the coal fire contemplating the fact that they were soon to be grand-parents. The room was cosy as they faced the same mantle shelf above the fireplace. The old clock ticked away reassuringly and the blue figurines stood at either end. Ernies reminder of a dear Mum, who was never far from his thoughts.

Pam had already decided that she would have her baby at her mothers house in Sunnydene. Everyone was over-joyed at the prospect as a new life was taking shape. Pam waited patiently, and did not miss the contact with Gerald her husband, who had been wetting the babys head at his local family pub in Efford, a suburb of Plymouth, from the day of its conception.

A BABY IS BORN

The birth came in late April, Spring was in its own joyous birth, bluebells had taken the place of golden daffodils in the fields and Pam gave birth to a son. The birth was too rapid, the family doctor was alarmed, she lost far too much blood. Swift action was needed, bricks were placed under the legs of the bed at the bottom end to elevate it. Pam was haemorraging. It took twenty four hours before the worry caused by the birth subsided enough for celebration. The first grandson had arrived, it made sisters into aunties and brothers into uncles.....and the chain of life continued. Phylis at fourty six, nursed Pam back to health and enjoyed feeding and caring for the baby that was named Colin. It took several months before Pam recovered enough from the traumatic birth to attempt to go home and cope alone. Pam still enjoyed daily contact with her Mum and Dad and could see no wrong in traveling to be with them, bringing baby Colin with her. White nappys waving in the breeze, toys packed away, with a kiss on the cheek she was sent home at the end of another enjoyable day. She was never eager to return home. The truth never really emerged as to why?

In October the family doctor was summoned once more. Jenny had appendicitis. The ambulance transported her to Freedom Fields Hospital for an urgent operation. As she recovered, although still young, her relationship with Leslie (Eddie) Edwards was getting serious, they were in love and asked for permission to marry. All the family were against such a young partnership, but Jenny could get around her Dad, so preparations began. Ernie worked overtime to foot the impending bill. They had wanted a spring wedding, when in December, after recovering from the appendix operation Jenny discovered she was pregnant. The wedding was brought forward to early January. It snowed, it was natures present of a white wedding!

St. Boniface Church had now seen two of Ernie and Phyls daughters married. Flats were hard to come by, so Ern decorated the front bedroom of their home as a bed-sit and Jenny commenced married life in Sunnydene. At sixteen it was still good fun to play snowball fights with your younger brothers. Phyl and Ern observed through the kitchen window as their three youngest off springs chased each other around in the deep snow. One of them was carrying another grandchild.

The grim winter gave way to glorious spring as it always does. Diane was now engaged to Michael, the television technician, she had changed employment and was working as chief cashier/bookkeeper for the prominent company of CIVIC TELEVISION which had recently done a take over of all STONES TELEVISION shops throughout the country. Dianes 'Bottom Drawer' was looking very healthy. She enjoyed restoration of old furniture and found it heartbreaking to discard anything. A trait which remained with her throughout her life, and I have a comfortable fondness when writing and reminiscing about Diane.

No one knows what is lying in wait for them on the rocky path of life. Each twist and turn not apparent at conception, it slowly unfolds with the signposts of life. Pam was taken ill, nothing serious was suspected at first, a touch of flu that lingered, stomach cramps that would not subside. Periods that kept her in bed for days. Initial examinations proved fruitless, then a totally wrong prognosis of pregnancy! One short month later, Ern and Phyl were so worried, they had spent hours at her flat, and she had seemed to show little signs of improvement. Gerald had assured them that he had done all that he could. Ern listened no longer, he summoned the top Gynecologist from Freedom Fields Hospital to attend. Within hours, Pam was admitted to hospital, she was operated on, and the grim truth was discovered. She had Cancer. She was twenty-five years old. It would prove to be terminal, fate decreed the inevitable. Ernie was passionately upset. He offered to donate any organ from his own body, he insisted, she must be saved this fate at all cost. His little Pamee. They had struggled to survive the 'BLITZ' but what ammunition do you use to fight this?

The operation consisted of a complete hysterectomy, followed by chemotherapy treatment, then she was discharged to the care of her parents, who had looked after baby Colin whilst she was in Hospital.

Jenny was asked if she and her husband could vacate their room for her sister. With the impending birth of her first child and pitifully few flats available, Jenny and Eddie moved in with her In-Laws. They had nine children, and lived in a three bedroomed house. Phyl and Ern did not tell Jenny the true extent of her sisters illness, they were concerned that the sad truth would affect her emotionally and therefore affect her unborn child.

THE NIGHTMARE BEGINS

Daily chemotherapy took its toll and gave no relief. An air of disbelief entered the home and surrounded the family. Diane supported Jenny, when on visits she would insist that everyone was going around with blinkers on, how could anyone ignore the fact that Pam was getting thinner and her skin had taken on a jaundice appearance. Diane placated Jenny, not allowing what they all KNEW to become truth by utterance. Pamela was dying.

Colin was a happy healthy baby, he crawled everywhere and provided the welcome relief from the constant gnawing fear that Pam was slipping away. Ernie spent time after work building a baby swing and relishing the chuckles that emanated from the baby. In time he walked unaided and adored his Nanna and Grandad, giving big appreciative hugs. Pam would smile weakly. No words were ever spoken, but she conveyed to Phyl how she wished Colin to look, and what he should wear when he reached five years old, as if instructing her mother in the event of her not being there. Their eyes would search each other out, but Pam never questioned and her Mother was never put on the spot to answer.

June 17th saw the birth of Jennys first son, Phyl and Erns second grandson. They tried to be jubilant and happy. Jenny sailed through the birth of Robert Lee, with no problems, thank God, as the family at Sunnydene were under that cloud that envelopes people who share their home with uncertainty.

Ern continued to work hard, providing anything Pam wanted. Gerald visited briefly each day, but the situation posed the necessity for him to live with his mother for the time being. It may not have been his fault, who can tell, but he could not sustain the sincerity of thought and deed that was needed in these circumstances. Fate had dealt a cruel blow on everyone concerned and Gerald drowned his sorrows in drink. He found no compassion in Phyl and Ern, they began to believe that he was partly to blame for what was happening to their daughter.

Brian and Derek were almost unaware of the impending doom that clutched the home they lived in. Things were made to seem as normal as possible. School, Football, scrapping in the street, conkers and alleys. Stringing girls up on trees when playing cowboys and Indians, playing with Colin in the garden, it all indicated normality.

The world, of course, careers on its way heedless of individuals ordeals and crisis.

Jenny and her son Robert Lee who was now a month old, seemed strong enough to know the truth. She was told of her sisters terminal cancer, it all seemed clear then why the secret had been kept from her. She got angry, then cried, she punched the air with her fist. She had gained a son and at any tick of the clock she was about to lose a sister.

TIME is a dirty four letter word, it robs us of our youth, our innocence, and yet it takes on a quality more valuable than all the worlds precious minerals when you are about to lose a loved one. Every waking moment in the days that followed, while she still had the strength, everyone indulged Pam. Jenny cut her hair, whilst she cradled her new nephew Robbie, a sweet small bundle with soft blonde curls. Diana not only kept her spirits up but took on the emotional welfare of the entire family on her twenty year old shoulders.

Ernie stayed the PROVIDER and Phyl found inner strength from somewhere to get her through each day. By not voicing the truth, she thought, it could never become fact. But it did become fact. In the dead of night on the 7th August Pamela Daisy slipped into a coma and out of this world.

She left Phyl and Ern with a void that was never filled, then, or in the years that followed.

The nightmare of the funeral, the flowers, the parting, and the discovery that she had never transferred her insurance policy to her husbands name, all took its toll. Phyl was heavily sedated. Colin, and his things were removed from the house by his father, under the guise that his Nanna needed rest. All was taken from them, no, not taken, stolen!

Relatives cared for Brian and Derek until some form of normality could be restored. The following month would have been their sisters twenty sixth birthday, it was the first of many hurdles that had to be overcome.

Christmas held little or no joy that year. Plymouth was now a completely rebuilt City with a superb shopping precinct complete with covered market, everywhere the lights and celebrations were in full swing. They were hollow celebrations at Sunnydene. Phyl returned from work each day and sat at the bottom of the stairs, alone in grief she cried. Ern did not, he had no outlet.

The new year however, heralded new hopes. Diane and Michael planned a March wedding, spirits could be lifted; Outwardly plans were in motion. Phyl and Ern stared out with empty eyes and tried to summon eager hearts.

St. Pauls Catholic Church, St. Budeaux was to be the venue. Michael was of Roman Catholic Faith and Diane learnt as much as she could about the religion she was marrying into. Michael was a solid reliable man, eleven years senior to Diane, he had suffered a sad childhood himself, without complaint. His acceptance of life and the cultivation of inner peace within the confines of a happy marriage was his ambition. Diane was twenty one when she said 'I Do'. They went off to an idyllic thatched cottage hideaway for their honeymoon. And yet another man had taken the place of THE PROVIDER!

With only two sons left at home, Brian at fifteen and Derek at twelve, there was every reason to plough on. Each year in coy affection, Ernie still presented Phyl with the box of hankies that had come to mean so much.

It was time for Brian to be contemplating a career, Ern wanted him to be a Plumber, believing it to be the trade of the future. Brian became a butcher! Such is life!

Grandad Westlake (Phyl's Dad) had entered his seventy sixth year. Phyl had cared for him whilst he lived next door, he had been witness to the sad events of the previous year. He was suddenly admitted to Hospital with a Prostrate Gland Problem. The operation proved too strenuous, he never recovered, just slipped peacefully away into the other world. Phyl was trying hard at the time to obtain visiting rights to little Colin. The ill feeling between the families was alive and kicking. Permission was refused. Grief, one way or another seemed endless.

GOODBYE WILLIAM

William George Westlake was buried at Weston Mill Cemetery, he shared a grave with Ada Beatrice and their daughter Beattie, the grave was only walking distance from where dear Pamela had been laid to rest the year before.

The only highlight of the year was the birth of Jenny's second child, a son. Trevor John who was born at Sunnydene. The baby had been due on American Independence Day, but arrived on the 7th July, three days later. Ern and Phyl were pleased to have the sound of a baby in the house once more. Baby Robbie was only one year old and the apple of his Grandads eye. The little lad had done so much in his young life to dull the pain of them not seeing Colin. Little Trevor cried constantly for six weeks until he was given an operation for a Hernia, so small and delicate, he needed constant care for months afterwards. But as time went on he turned out to be a real grinner, and would smile at anything.

The months went by and soon there was the makings of a new year on the doorstep. The family at Sunnydene decided it was time to move on. They put in for a transfer, mainly because 5 Sunnydene still held the sadness within its walls and refused to let go. A prefab in Kingstamerton became available, they moved with the echoes of good wishes expressed from neighbours. Tears were shed at the parting. Their joy of life returned, there was an air of purpose, and Diane gave birth to Phyl and Erns first Grand-daughter. Michelle Patricia arrived in this world on the 18th October 1965.

Ernie was now fifty three, Phyl was fourty nine, they had amassed three grandsons and one grand daughter. Ern was still working for the Cooperation as a painter, his old habits were still with him. Ask Ernie for any shade of paint for any job and he could disappear into his shed and mix it in a flash, if he did not have it, he could guarantee to have it by the weekend! Phyl had taken a job as a home help, it was a little bit of pin-money, she would meet up with Erns sister Jessie on pay day, which was Thursday, and they would go to the market or any sales that were on and enjoy spending their pay packets. In one of the houses she was working at Phyl had just finished polishing the passageway, when she slipped and fell. The shock to her spine made her involuntary wet herself. Embarrassed by her plight, she struggled home. Days later the pain was still evident and her head would not stay upright without help. A hospital stay of fourteen days followed, in traction for most of the time, Phyl was depressed. Ern showed up each day with the predictable posy of flowers he had picked along the way. He could spot a flower in a bramble hedge from a hundred paces, he had the knack of putting wild daisys or primroses in a bunch and surrounding them with leaves from the plant to make the sweetest of posys. Ernie did it all his life. His mother was the early recipient, but now always with a coy smile, it was Phylis who received the posys, as he dropped it in her lap he would say "Er yar!"

The same year, whilst Phyl was at home convalescing, the family suffered another setback. Ern had a nervous breakdown. The doctor diagnosed it as delayed shock manifesting itself because of Pams death. The whole family could not believe that the PROVIDER had thrown in the towel, but he preferred to stay locked away in the bedroom. No hurt could reach him there. Phyl and Ern sat together recuperating in the garden that he had cultivated around the prefab, but if anyone approached he would scurry indoors. Visits from grandchildren, hugs from daughters, offers of help from sons, nothing would break the wall around the world he put himself into.

Just as suddenly as it appeared as a cloud around him, months later he snapped out of it, worst of all, he would not discuss his feelings, not even with Phyl.

With annual regularity Jenny provided another grandson. January 10th, 1966 saw the arrival of Shaun Paul, who was born to Jen in the little flat in 28 Oxford Avenue, just ten houses up from where Jenny herself had been born, as independent as always, she was alone at the time of the birth. Her third child born on her third anniversary. Phyl enjoyed being a Mum, but at times like this, it was a real concern. The young family moved after Shauns birth to a larger three bedroomed house with a garden, but throughout her young marriage, it was beginning to be obvious to Phyl and Ern as onlookers, that she was the PROVIDER in this union. Eddies plans were 'Pie in the sky'. Ern listened to his son-in-law and absorbed, whilst Jenny took jobs that fitted in with the routine of a young familys timetable of feeding, washing and bedtime. Because of her husbands erratic working career, Jen often had to rely on Derek to be the babysitter, he enjoyed the time they spent together, and Phyl and Ern who found Derek quite studious and introvert were pleased that he could share his thoughts and feelings for life with his older sister. They had a good relationship and Jenny's house was always bubbling over with laughter, when the pair of them would imitate the comedians of the day. Peter Cook and Dudley Moore were their favourites, or Monty Python and most sketches could be learned and copied to great effect.

Brian and Derek had been up to then a couple of teenage boys who were usually blamed for things, even if they were innocent. But guilty or not Ern would never have a bad word said about either. Sometimes the activities of the Johnsey boys would create much frustration amongst the local constabulary. Ern understood the boys from this respect, he had been a bit of a devil himself in his time, and he liked to think that his sons were a chip off the old block. But Ern couldn't help himself, it was bred in him, and he meant no harm, and did none. But you can be sure no rabbit died of old age at Plym Bridge when Ernie and his brothers were young. They were often chased by the local copper themselves.

Phyls motherly support was needed greatly the following year. Derek was now working, indulging his passion for engines, working in a garage. He learnt to drive at the age of fifteen, moving cars around the forecourt. He had witnessed his parents sadness and had not had the maturity to cope with it, so he spent increasingly more hours up at Jennys house. There was laughter and fun, and they had a good relationship as brother and sister, and besides he was never asked all the time to "Get yer hair cut!" Jenny was a great cook. Plenty of Bacon Sandwiches and mugs of tea.

Another year, another baby. Jenny was pregnant yet again, and so was Diane. Brian was courting a young girl called Christine, his first real love. With the imminent birth of two new grand-children, the future looked brighter. Christmas had renewed its meaning and picnics at Plym Valley revived for everyone. Diane had suffered a miscarriage, so carrying this baby was important. Michelle was now a sweet toddler. Jennys babe was due in February, but Phyl and Ern held no fears for her, she had babies like shelling peas. Diane's baby was due in April, but she regularly voiced her own fears that the baby inside her was not strong and several times she panicked when she thought she could not feel its heart beat. Phyl assured her it was only motherly concern and that everything would be alright, but the stress could be detected on her young face.

Granddad Johns taught all his grand-children funny rhymes, card games, and clever tricks with milk bottle tops. He was in his element when children were around and they adored him. Sweet little Michelle spent hours with Nanny in the garden picking flowers for her own Mummy.

True to the annual prediction, Jennys baby was born on 11th February 1967. She had been convinced all along that she carried this baby differently, indicating to all intense and purposes that it would be a girl! It was no surprise to Phyl, when she visited the next day to be encouraged by little Robbie and Trevor to "Come and look at our Wendy Lisa Nanny!!!" with eye brows raised, Phyl knew that her daughter Jenny would have her work cut out to explain that the child was a boy. Raymond Leslie Keith was still referred to as Wendy Lisa for a few weeks after until the children got used to the idea that they had a brother.

In the meantime baby Raymond, snug in his young mothers arms had fists clenched to fight the world. Phyl and Ernie were delighted with the ever growing family. More grandchildren to love. Jenny produced good looking babies with blonde curls. Ern was glad that heritage had everything to do with that!

Robbie the eldest at 3 years old was grandads card playing mate. Trevor at 2 years old, smiled at everything and gave nanny a reason to keep the biscuit barrel full. Shaun was now 1 year old, a lively funny inventive child who kept everyone on their toes. To complete this bunch baby Raymond, a funny little character who grew to amuse the whole family. They were like peas in a pod, never knowing a time when there was'nt all four of them. Jenny was their PROVIDER at the grand old age of twenty one.

Life is never a straight line, more a zig zag! and as long as you did everything with a passion and gave love to your family Ernie was happy to impart what he had learned in his life. He was a strong man, six feet tall with strong shoulders and big hands and no one messed with Ernie Johns.

DIANE'S LOSS

Shortly after the safe arrival of Jennys healthy son, Diane was admitted to hospital. The doctor was now sharing her concern for the unborn child. The heartbeat got fainter until it could be detected no longer, they induced the birth and Diane knew she would have to endure the labour pains with nothing to hold at the end of it. Phyl experienced every contraction and was relieved when Michael broke the news that it was all over. They had sadly lost a baby girl. The child was baptised Helen and they returned to their neat little home in Horsham Lane, Honicknowle.

It took another two years before Diane and Michael had another child, a little girl. Jane Catherine, born 29th April 1968. The joy of holding this blonde haired bundle compensated for the loss of loving and raising baby Helen. Caroline Jennifer completed the Pile family with her arrival a year later on the 30th June 1969. The winters and summers seemed endless times of growing children. Visiting Nanny and Grandad Johns was always a highlight of these young lives. Grandad would always have an enormous capacity to amuse little people and Nanny would make buns and knit fancy jumpers for them all. Their role as Grandparents was a very rewarding one.

Phyl and Erns youngest daughter Jenny was now a chef at the Grand Hotel on Plymouth Hoe. Tragedy in her marriage had now put her in the role of breadwinner for her family of four young sons, she never had another child, and Derek became almost a permanent resident at her house, helping in any way he could for his sister. Looking after the children when necessary, and making endless pots of tea whilst they enjoyed therapeutic evaluation of the world and its purpose, they never solved all the worlds problems, but had fun trying.

In 1974, Derek announced to all the family that he was going to emigrate to greener pastures, namely New Zealand. A family dinner at the Continental Hotel to farewell the youngest son and in no time at all he was gone .Duneden would be his new home.

He took with him some very special memories. The previous year he had been best man at his brother Brians marriage at St. Budeaux Parish Church. Brian married Christine, his first real serious girlfriend. He could also recall the memory of his twenty first birthday party, what a night that was. They ended the night in the newly opened Pier West Bar of the Holiday Inn that Jenny was then managing at the tender age of twenty four.. Drinks flowed and Dereks tipple of rum and black was downed in pint glasses....... a celebration with a difference. A 21st present from Jen of a tankard with the symbol of Sir Francis Drake standing proudly on Plymouth Hoe was hoped would remind him of where he came from. Derek needed nothing but what he held in his heart to remind him and Ern was happy for implanting it there.

The nest was now empty, how could it be so.

Brians wife Christine was overjoyed when she gave birth to a son eighteen months after their marriage. The birth of Andrew heralded the start for Phylis of continued heart problems. She had been feeling tired for some time, but put it down to her part time job of Home Help. There was always something to get on with, and if she returned from work at lunch times and promptly fell asleep in the chair, through weariness, it annoyed her greatly. She told Ern not to worry that she was just feeling a bit off colour. At the time of baby Andrews arrival into the world, Phyl would not be deterred from visiting her new grandson. She congratulated an overjoyed Brian, kissed Christine who was sitting up in her hospital bed glowing with pride when Phyl, absorbing the sight of the baby came over very faint, she asked for some fresh air. When she got outside, she promptly collapsed. The nursing staff helped her to her feet and took her in a room where she could rest.

A few days later she suffered a massive heart attack, Ernie and the family were told to expect the worst, she would not last the night.

Phyl knows she was dying at the time and distinctly remembers a tunnel of light, she paused and looked back down from high up in the room and saw doctors and nurses attending the body she had vacated back on the bed. She continued to move on up towards the light when a voice halted her weightless journey. It was Dereks voice, backed up with Erns, they were both calling for her to come back and please don't go. Derek was in Fiji when this happened, he had received a telegram and could do very little but think of home and a mother that may already be gone whilst he was reading the urgent typewritten words on the telegram he held in his hands.

In England, the night of waiting was over. Ern was told that although the next fourty eight hours were crucial, there was positive hope that she would pull through. The tears that were shed by everyone during the night in private contemplation were never measured or recorded only in the hearts of this close family.

Phyl remained in the Intensive Care Unit of Freedom Fields Hospital for another two weeks, and a further week on a medical ward. The nurses were praised for such unstinting care and devotion to patient comfort. She was eventually discharged to the care of a very nervous Ernie. She could do nothing for herself, that was the time when the **NEW AGE MAN** was born prematurely! Ern did the housework, washing, cooking and cleaning, and give him his due, he did it well.

The recovery was a long term thing, with small milestones for Phyl in regaining her own independence. It never really occurred, because the love that Ernie showered on his wife, wrapping her in cotton wool and cosseting her, made her less and less likely to achieve it. Eventually there was nothing she could do but contentedly submit to his insistence at taking over everything. After several months there was no argument, Ernie was the **PROVIDER, CARER**, and the Emotional support for Phyl, and their pattern for the autumn years of their life was set, and set proper.

Derek then returned home from overseas bringing with him the girl who would be his future wife. Ernie and Phylis made her welcome, and Christy soon learned that the Johnsys have a code of practice, however questionable that cannot be reversed. They pull together like metal filings towards a magnet. It was difficult to enter, and there were no guidelines of what was required of an '**OUTSIDER**'.

Derek married Christy in the presence of a small family group at the Registry Office in Plymouth, and very soon their first child was on its way. It was to be Ern and Phyls tenth grandchild. Phyl was sixty years old by then and Ernie a spritely sixty four.

Families are apt to part and go their own ways eventually and Jenny had been making plans for some time to emigrate too Australia with her four young sons,, without consulting anyone. She had been a Chef, a Silver Service Waitress, and also done P.R. and Reception work in her varied career, whilst raising and providing for her four sons. She even joined the WRAF reserves, and Phyl and Ern looked after the boys when Jenny did a Sunday training session for that, it gave her a good social life, and Ern and Phyl knew that she enjoyed letting her hair down when she had the chance. A Training weekend in Scotland and the journey on the train through the lake district and onto Scotland would cement Jenny's love of Scotland.

At the time that she was finalising her plans to travel to Australia, she had been running her own business for two years, selling and supplying fresh fish that she purchased in the daily fish auctions on Plymouth Barbican. It was a difficult start but she was soon accepted at the early morning sales, and very soon the hammer would drop and the sale would go to "Blondie" and it was a job where she could set her own hours, taking the boys with her on School Holidays. They were good little workers like their mother.

Diane worked with Jenny two days a week and they particularly loved Thursdays as that was the day when the round that Jen had established took them out around where their Mum and Dad lived. A cup of tea and hot soup was always waiting and welcome, and whilst they enjoyed the lunch break, Phyl and Ern would select some fish for tea from the van parked outside.

Ern was always proud of the fact that Jenny seemed to have inherited his fighting spirit and optimistic nature. She had seen and endured enough in her young life, but her plans to remove herself and their four grandsons twelve thousand miles away met with opposition.

But Ernies daughter who had certainly inherited his traits showed the spirit that he had been so proud of by sticking to her guns. She sold up and prepared for whatever awaited her '**DOWN UNDER**'.

Phyl and Ern thought they would never see her again. Ern even said that if she wanted to be on her own for a while, why didn't she move to Scotland, she could come back from there!!!But Jenny had chosen Australia after another night alone when the children were asleep, holding an atlas in her hands she looked up for spiritual guidance and made a pact that wherever the Atlas fell open..thats where she would take her children for a new life! Derek and Christy gave sensible advise. Derek was now a confident seasoned traveler having moved from New Zealand to Fiji and then to Australia. He had met Christy whilst working in a holiday resort in the mountains north of Melbourne, Australia. She was a New Zealand girl whose parents lived in Auckland.

During the year of Jennys departure from English shores, Brian and Christine had been overjoyed with the birth of their little girl Helen Mary Johns on March 29th 1976. Andrew David was about to celebrate his second birthday, so with one of each their family was now complete. Dereks wife Christy also gave birth on July 18th to a son, Samuel Bede Johns. The JOHNSY clan was increasing with every year.

GOODBYE TO JENNY

Diane and Jenny had spent the final days in excited contemplation of what was to come, they took the children for a picnic on Saltram beach, just outside Plymouth, and whilst they played, they chatted about the past, the present and most importantly, the future. They would miss each other, there was no question about that. Diane decided she would accompany the family to Heathrow for the farewell.

Heathrow Airport was alive and buzzing that day in August 1976 and very exciting for four young grandsons who had travelled overnight on a train from Plymouth to London playing cards with Grandad. When little Raymond grew tired he was hoisted up onto the luggage rack to sleep whilst the train truddled along on its journey. Much was left unsaid, tears flowed freely as they held each other and with four children, four suitcases and four hundred dollars they watched as Jenny and the boys went out of sight into the departure lounge to board the Qantas Jet. With no family or friends at the other end Ern wondered what would become of his youngest daughter.

For Phyl and Ern God had provided two new lives that year, and removed five lives out of reach. They still considered themselves lucky. Diane visited regularly, always bringing flowers that were in season, freshly baked cakes and three well loved grand daughters who enjoyed making up songs and performing for Nanny and Grandad. The compensations in the Autumn years were in abundance. Diane would always be the anchor, her visits were relished and the pleasure shared.

That year had certainly seen some changes, Phyl and Ernie had moved into a small bungalow in a row of elderly residents units. Ern never by any stretch of the imagination considered himself an elderly resident! Newly retired from full-time work, he couldn't wait to secure part-time employment. At sixty six he had a lifestyle he enjoyed, a wife he loved, and children that knew where he was if they needed him. He enjoyed getting out of the house when his chores were complete and his Phyl made comfortable. After ten years of this regime' he had convinced her that she could not do anything, let alone attempt it. Her angina attacks would be a sign for him to spring into action, for he knew exactly what to do.

They celebrated their Wedding Anniversarys with small coach trips, usually up the coast. Jokingly Ernie would say "I remember my wedding day as if it was only yesterday and you know what a bloody horrible day yesterday was!" He was the eternal joker, always finding humour even if none was intended or wanted, which would sometimes upset the '**OUTSIDERS**'.

DESTINATION
NEW ZEALAND -
FAREWELL SAM

As always, just when you feel comfortable with 'Your Lot' someone rocks the boat. This time it was Christy. Dereks wife said she wanted to return to New Zealand and her own family. He understood, but financially could not oblige just at that time. Derek searched around for better, more lucrative employment and landed a job in Germany that offered excellent pay. It would take him three months to get what they needed to secure his wifes dream of going home. During his absence, Ern and Phyl watched as young Christy set up a separate lifestyle for herself and her baby son Sam. No one can explain what occurs in the hearts of people that lead them apart, but on Dereks return from Germany, the separation was finalised and he moved in with Brian and Chris. In the meantime Christy obtained the fare from her parents in New Zealand and flew home with no goodbyes. Phyl and Ern were not given the opportunity to kiss baby Sam goodbye, worst of all they didn't understand why. They never saw Sam again. Learning many years later that Christy had moved to America and married an American.

Phyl and Ern hated standing by, watching their youngest son swallow himself up in his own misery. A family conference was in order, and with approval from Derek they came up with the suggestion of sending him out to Jenny in Australia. Two years had elapsed and she was happily settled in Perth, Western Australia. They all knew that Der and Jen always got on well, it would be just the thing to get him back on his feet again. A flight to Singapore and then passenger accommodation on a Russian Liner was quickly arranged for Derek. He was off again.

ARRIVAL DOWN UNDER

In England, they waited expectantly for the descriptive letter from Jenny that would describe the arrival of the ship in Fremantle Harbour early one February morning. Jen and the four boys had stood on the highest peak in Fremantle, on top of Monument Hill to be exact, at 6 a.m. and watched the ship off shore, bathed in early morning sunlight. The air was already warm around them, not a breath of breeze anywhere. The blue sea sparkled like diamonds against an azure sky.

Robbie, Trevy, Shauny and Raysie were even more excited than Jenny at Dereks arrival. He was their Uncle, someone to play cricket with. Someone who would remember all the card games that Granddad used to play. They missed their grandparents very much. Jenny wrote with vivid detail, knowing that her Mum and Dad would hang on every word, and they did.

The scene was a busy one, Fremantle Docks was a huge place, and the young family having descended from Monument Hill and entered the Docks area were now hanging over the railings to watch as the ship berthed. All sets of eyes scanned the decks for a familiar sight, and way up on the deck near the top of the ship, they spotted him. He was already looking at them. Frantic waving began. The wait for custom clearance seemed ages, and then he appeared, tall and thin with one battered suitcase and lonely eyes.

It did not take long to renew the old feelings. The drive up the Freeway from Fremantle to Perth was full of chatter, messages from Mum and Dad were exchanged and the boys wanted to know how their favourite football teams were doing that season.Manchester United was still their favourite. A knocking from the back axle interrupted the lively conversation. On arrival at the house in Nabawa Street, Riverton, Der with his mechanical knowledge soon discovered the differential had snapped! He spent his first weekend underneath Jens car with a bunch of tools, covered in oil from the rear axle and being fed bacon sandwiches and mugs of tea from Jens kitchen. Ah...lovely.....life had returned to normal!!!

Phyl and Ern, back in England, read and re-read the letters that told of these events. Diane and Brian were given graphic details with every visit. Dianes change in career was now secure. They had moved house from a lovely big three bedroomed property in Plympton, to the rolling green countryside of Cornwall. They had taken up residence in Gunnislake, in a charming character packed bungalow, with 'Potential'. The Beech trees framed an archway above the gate that had a plaque on it bearing the name CARFRAE. They were smitten. So what if it did have a bit of damp here and there, it was nothing that Michael couldn't fix.....and anyway....look at the view? People paid thousands for a chance of a view like that. Ern thought it was a silly move, but Phyl said reassuringly "Well, its their life" But lets face it, he hadn't quite come to grips with that fact.

Moving to Gunnislake enabled Diane to secure work in the Restaurant of St. Mellion Golf & Country Club, situated between Callington and Saltash. Michael worked from home after building a workshop which could look up into the kitchen so he could see when the kettle was on. The girls were growing away and each now showing signs of artistic talents. Michael had wanted to retire to the country and paint with oils, but as time went on his painting became essentially restricted to the upkeep and maintenance of the property.

1979

This was to be a year that they would not forget. Airmail letters had been the only contact Phyl and Ern had with their daughter and son 'DOWN UNDER', when out of the blue one day came the offer that gave them the trip of a lifetime. Jen and Der said they could supply the cost of a return air ticket if they could get the funds together for the other one. This offer called for a pot of tea and the company of Di and Bri to discuss at great lengths the fors and againsts of such a holiday. Eventually the invitation was accepted and plans were underway for Phyl and Ern to experience life in Australia first hand. They were going to stay with Jenny and the boys for three months. The boys were now fifteen, fourteen, thirteen and twelve respectively. They were eager beavers, with tanned happy faces and they were certainly looking forward to this visit.

Brian, Diane and Erns sister Jessie accompanied them to Heathrow Airport. Diane had been so many times to see people off that she wore a special skirt for the occasion, here in after referred to as her 'AIRPORT SKIRT'!

Phyl and Ern had never flown before and did not know what to expect. They boarded the aircraft with the anticipation of small children on a Sunday school outing. They held hands for mutual support. The plane soared high into the sky, Phyl held her breath and Ern closed his eyes, and when the plane leveled out and commenced the long haul towards their first re-fuel stop, confidence returned. Cabin staff put a tray of delicious looking food in front of them and the question "Would you care for a drink?" Met with the reply from Ernie of "Make mine a double!".

The fascination of the newness of the experience did not wear off, here they were flying at thirty thousand feet, closer to the Main Provider than they had ever envisaged in all their years. Having left family on the ground worrying about them, they were now winging their way towards family at the other end of the world.

Ernie ate and drank everything on offer, by the time they were descending for the first re-fuel stop he was very merry and slightly high in his own way! The captains voice came over the air with a message that unfortunately one engine had failed, Ernie showed no alarm...after all.. they had another one didn't they? The message went on to say that they would experience a delay at Bahrain until the new engine could be installed.

The passenger lounge at Bahrain was dull dusty and guarded with dark menacing looking figures that held everyone at bay with machine guns. Phyl and Ern had only seen things like this on the films.

Ern was worried about Phyl, she needed water to take her tablets and there seemed no way of making oneself known to these foreigners! Ernie decided he would get a drink for Phyl as the hours were ticking by and there did not look like any immediate hope of reboarding the plane for quite a long time. He tried to leave the lounge area only to be confronted by a loaded rifle, "Must go back, Must go back, you stay" said the man holding the rifle, well you can't argue with a loaded gun. A dejected Ernie sat down and behaved himself.

The heat was oppressive and so when the call to **BOARD** was heard over the loudspeaker, everyone rushed for the door eager to escape the confinement.

Strapped into their seats once more the plane truddled down the run way gathering speed until it had sufficient momentum to get it off the ground, it shuddered and shook, no one on the plane knew why at that stage, but Ernie was beginning to think it was a flight into hell. Settled once more with more complimentary whisky and replenished with food, Ernie looked across to Phyl and said "Well if we got a go, we'll go together, and as we are this high up we aint got far to go!"

An in-flight movie passed some time away and they talked once more to an elderly lady they had met on the ground, her destination was Melbourne, where like Phyl and Ern she was to be met by relatives. The experience on the ground at Bahrain had frightened her.

They all laughed together at the sight of an Arab gentleman who had entered the waiting room at Bahrain, he had just arrived from another country and swaned on through past everyone, he was dressed in flowing robes and a wonderful turban. Behind him in single file walked six beautiful girls, slim and tall wearing soft flowing fabrics that touched the ground, they were decorated with many gold bangles, their faces were hidden with yasmaks but their eyes were dark and deep and everyone watched in awe of this procession. These topics and more held their interest until the plane was approaching Bombay.

THE BOMBAY SKID

As they approached the runway the Captains voice came over the air once more. "We are sorry to have to inform you, but during take off at Bahrain we burst all the tyres on our landing wheels! We have radioed ahead for assistance, please do not be alarmed if you see Fire Engines and Ambulances lining the runway....it is only a safety precaution." The plane then circled the airport to discharge any reserve fuel, they used the emergency landing techniques, and while this drama unfolded in the cockpit of the aircraft, Phyl and Ern held hands tightly and as tears ran down their cheeks they prayed they would get back on the ground in one piece.

The plane touched down skidding and screeching as it went until it finally came to a hault further down the runway than anticipated. All was silent inside until passengers looked around them and a loud cheer went up as collectively they shook hands. The Captain came through with the crew when they knew the danger of a crash and fire on impact was confirmed. A loud cheer and joint voices in harmony singing "FOR HE'S A JOLLY GOOD FELLOW" was heard inside the plane whilst outside the Fire Engines and Ambulances had reached the stationary plane. Phyl was sure now that if she did not suffer an attack after all that lot, then there was hope for her yet.

They descended down the steps of the aircraft with wobbly knees and saw for the first time the extent of the damage, it was now evident that it was by sheer pilot skill that they had landed at all. When they reached the lounge area at Bombay, there was a comradeship amongst the passengers who had come through these traumas together. The plane was now hopelessly overdue. Jenny and Derek in Australia had been ringing Perth airport constantly for information, but no other details other that the lateness of its arrival were given. They would have to wait for their Mum and Dad to find out the full story.

The waiting began!!!!

For some passengers, this had all been too much, they refused to reboard the same plane when the time came and the repairs completed. Phyl and Ern were lost, they were in an alien environment, and just went with the flow. They did board the aircraft for the third time and just hoped for the best and lets face it, what else could happen now!!!!

WE MADE IT!

Perth was in sight and no disaster warnings had come over the air from the pilot, so there was much rejoicing. The pilot did finally speak, he thanked everyone that had decided to stay with it, and he also said a special thank you to the many passengers who had made a collection for him in appreciation of their safe landing under such trying conditions. He was grateful and wished them a pleasant and enjoyable stay in Perth Western Australia, he announced that they would be landing in approximately twenty minutes and the outside temperature on landing would be a comfortable twenty eight degrees. He finished by saying "Thank you for flying British Airways".

A safe landing followed by trouble free customs regulations, they walked with a full airport trolley through the automatic doors and into the waiting arms of the family 'Down Under'.

Jenny and Derek drove them through the Australian sunshine to Jens house in Foxwood Court, Langford, which would be home for the next three months. It was lovely, but after describing their fear and adventure during the hazardous flight, all they wanted was a cup of tea and a comfortable bed. Both were provided in that order. They slept all day and were quite disorientated when they awoke.

The next three months went by in a whirlwind of Bar-B-Ques, family fun, getting to know everyone again. Helping young Raymond prepare for his first date. He had planned to take a girl to a local Disco, and Phyl and Ern watched as he slicked his hair and looked real snazzy in his leather waistcoat. Click went the camera to capture the moment. But there were many moments like this, too numerous to mention, some moments were captured with the wink of an eye and held in their hearts forever. Ernie made himself useful in Jennys big garden, digging, planting new and unusual plants, he loved the exotic colours. The regular car rides with Derek up to Kings Park which majestically overlooked all of Perth City were enthusiastically savoured. Derek, very conveniently lived next door, so card nights or scrabble games were easy to organise. There were endless pots of tea and chats about this and that. Ern and Phyl found comfortable allies in Jen and Ders neighbours Faye and Alan, and in appreciation of the new friendship, Faye put on one of her famous Bar-B-Que nights. The food was plentiful, and the conversation flowed as the sun went down over the large aviary in her back garden. Ernie got drunk that night, merrily so. Phyl went on home to bed, she did not like to see Ernie like this, he got very amorous on these occasions, so she was sure she would be asleep when he finally crawled into bed. But Ernie in his innocent fashion stayed with Derek and Jenny and all the family drinking to his hearts content. He was on holiday. He conveyed to Derek that night, just how proud he was of him and that it was a comfort to know that he was sorting his life out and to know that his job with the West Australian Water Board had prospects, well, that called for another drink!!!

The trio swayed home in the early hours of the morning, Jenny with one of Dads arms slung around her neck and Derek on the other side supporting him, they giggled and tripped over the step, giggled again and tripped over another step, then as Jenny was putting the key in the door Ern kept telling everyone to Shush! So we started talking in hushed whispers, heavens knows why, every man and his dog was asleep. We closed the front door behind us and very soon we were all asleep. If Ernie had any amorous intent, he had forgotten it by the time his head hit the pillow.

The sunny days continued, and on the days when Jenny was at work, Phyl and Ern would enjoy doing the family wash. The thrill of being able to hang out the washing, then pick it in within the hour ready to iron, never failed to impress Ernie. He loved the sunshine, and the time he spent in the garden paid dividends. Ernie also built a larger aviary for Jennys expanding collection of birds. There was always the Cooee....over the fence to Der when he was at home to let him know the kettle was on!

Jens boys had grown up in the years they had spent in Australia before Phyl and Erns visit, so it was a time for renewing relationships. Weekends, all the four of them worked for the SUNDAY TIMES newspaper company, selling the papers. They would try and beat each other with the amounts sold because commission was paid on quantity of sales. They would arrive home at different

Mum & Dad on Holiday in Australia 1979

times and pour all the loose change from their pockets counting the tips and seeing who had made the most. It was very lucrative employment for four so young. In future years Trevor went on to work as a Junior Accountant for the same Newspaper Company.

Ernie and Phyl enjoyed being part of all these things. The boys were encouraged to bank half their earnings by their mother, which stood them in good stead in later years.

The day of the opening of the big shopping centre at KARAWARA was also a fond memory for them both. With loaded trolleys they scooped up lots of opening day bargains. Then a short ride home to check out the bargains over a cup of tea.

Two months had elapsed when Ern got mail from home from his sister Jessie. She explained that Erns younger sister Beatrice May had passed away, she was sixty one years old. He quietly got changed and went for a walk, he dealt with most things in that way, in quiet contemplation. He walked and thought of the commencement of the family, winding like a river, then came the families that followed him, the daughters and sons who thronged the house until they grew up and passed out into the world, then there was another generation, and more children down the years.

Time was now short, just a few weeks to go before they would be winging their way back home to England. The next opportunity that occurred was midweek, a trip up the Swan River on a wine cruise was organised. They boarded the glass topped boat at Barrack Street Jetty, and slowly meandered up river. Points of interest were observed on the way accompanied with glasses of wine from different wineries. The tasting session went on all day. The destination was a Lodge up river that had historical importance, anything before 1900 in Western Australia had historical importance. The country was very new in comparison to England. A chicken luncheon served in the cellars of The Haughton Valley Winery was enjoyed. It was Moondyne Joe country and Ernie had enjoyed the books Jenny had sent him about this convivial character. There had been a family link way back on the family tree, but Ernie had never been able to establish it totally.

Another trip out to Wave Rock, roughly six hundred miles from Perth left them speechless. Phyl and Ern had never in their lives envisaged such long straight roads, with scrub and bush looking like it needed a good drink. Wave Rock itself was a magnificent sight, the natural formation towered above them in the shape of a surfing wave, unusual and awe inspiring. Man could never build the like, and they were looking at something that had stood there for millions of years, it was hard to absorb.

Der took them on another trip up to a farm in the bush to friends of his. Jenny worked that weekend. Ernie was so surprised at all he saw, and always grateful for the opportunity. Phyl was just happy to be with Ernie.

The last week came, numerous car rides to Kings Park to take some lovely photos amongst the acres of wildflowers.

The everlastings were in profusion that year, these would be lovely memories in the years that followed.

Their minds were saturated with places, faces and situations by the time they came to board the Jumbo Jet which would transport them home. Jennys friend was a Sergeant in the West Australian Police Force and although he kept a low profile during Phyl and Erns visit, Peter came up trumps with a suitable selection of gifts for them to take back to England with them. He even wrote a personal reference written in a humorous vein regarding their qualities as the Upstairs/**Downstairs** staff.

The parting was once again sad, the journey home much more comfortable than the outward flight, and let's face it, they knew what to expect. They were greeted at Heathrow Airport as the thousand couple to walk through the barrier, a few details collected for a later brochure and they were on their way out through the automatic doors and into the arms of the English contingent.

Diane, in her airport skirt drove up with Mike to meet them in one car and Brian and Chris and family in the other car. They separated them for the journey back to Plymouth so each car could get all the exciting details. However Mike took the scenic route back and arrived hours later than Bri. Ernie was a worried man, would he ever learn to relax.

Life back in the bungalow in Chard Road reverted to normal. Jessie, who had been doing Erns little cleaning job on the Hoe during his absence stayed on and he got himself a few hours work in a local doctors surgery that worked out well. And Brian left for Germany to find out how the prospects for Bricklayers compared over there to the conditions in England.

Bri came home again after a few months to tell Chris that he could provide better for her and the kids if he worked in Germany. He always returned home for Christmas. When he arrived back bearing gifts for the Christmas of 1980, Chris had made her mind up that she was going back with him. They sold up and moved to Neuburg-ab-donnan in West Germany. Brian worked in Munich, and his day was a long one which involved much travelling. Chris wrote home to her own Mum and also Bri's Mum telling them of her long lonely days, she was trying hard to speak the language. The children adapted easily and very soon photos of them in National Costume were arriving on the doorstep. Money was not plentiful in the beginning, but Chris made do. They bought a big pine double bed and all four of them slept in it for a month. Andrew was seven and Helen five. They got together a home of fine furniture eventually, and the children spoke fluent German.

Almost two years had gone by. One day Phyl and Ern, having done their chores in the neat little bungalow made a pot of tea, set it all out on a tray and took it outside so they could sit out the back garden, as they had done on many occasions in the sunshine. Phyl was busy knitting dollys, and Ern, after cutting up the foam filling to go inside the dollys, had read his newspaper for a while. He had been using a matchstick to poke around in his ear, he was deep in thought, when he suddenly said "Jen and Der are living in Australia. Bri is in Germany. What will we do if Di goes away?"

Phyl had never contemplated loosing all of them, surely one family would stay close. It would have to be Diane. Her deep rooted love of England would hold her, and what's more Diane clung on to things that were eminently disposable, such as cards, bits of string, plastic bags, fancy wrapping paper, pretty boxes and tins......she would never move......would she?

Diane and Michael were now well established at 'Carfrae'. Their girls were now young women. Michelle was eighteen, Jane at fifteen and Caroline fourteen, they had a young maturity. Ern and Phyl loved them dearly. They always thought up something exciting for Grandads birthday.

They liked clothes, much like other young girls, but they still found time to enjoy activities with their Mum. Making chocolate eggs at Easter, or handmade greetings cards, this family was talented. Michelle was making a name for herself with her expertise with Fimo modeling clay, she could mould anything from a small hedgehog to a full scale model. She was trying her hand at running her own business, with financial backing from her parents. She had found a small shop in an arcade in Tavistock and stocked the shop with her collection. Jane showed a promising artistic streak and had a wonderful flair with oil crayons. Caroline who had always been in love with a horse, was beginning to shape up as an excellent student.

So all was well with the Pile family. Diane had been promoted to Restaurant Manageress at St. Mellion Golf and Country Club, and enjoyed organizing the many functions. Michael continued to work from home, either in the workshop, or on the extension that he was planning to build. Michael even found some time to do oil painting which he loved, but was never satisfied with his results, even when they were perfect!!!

Summers in the garden at 'Carfrae' were a haze of soft scented flowers and pale green Beech trees that seemed to enclose the entire cottage. Diane would bake, and the sounds from the garden would waft up through the open window. Phyl and Ern loved it when Michael suggested on many occasions, to pick them up and drive them down for the day. Caroline would have high jinks with Grandad, who she nicknamed 'THE MAN IN BLACK'. Caroline would place a straw hat on Grandads head and get him to ride Magic, the pony. Ernie would do anything to hear the girls giggle. Nanny would sit happily in the garden sipping tea and eating the output from the kitchen, Di liked to entertain, and got great pleasure from her parents visits. She would send them back home with armfuls of flowers from the garden, and tasters from the kitchen.

Following a two year stint working in Germany, Bri and Chris were thinking of coming back to England to live. Germany had many advantages, one was the quick access to Austria for weekend trips. There was always somewhere to go and something to do, and the young family made the most of it. However, putting all the advantages to one side, They both missed their familys very much. Chris came home with the children in July 1983, and Brian returned in October the same year, after organising the storing of their furniture until a convenient collection date could be organised. Housing in Plymouth was to prove the biggest problem, so they became homeless and were allocated a small flat in Battery Street, near the Millbay Road red light district. They thought it would only be short term until the council offered them a house. They eventually stayed in the flat for eight weeks before a house was allocated to them. Whilst they lived in the Battery Street flat, Andrew spent many hours looking out of the window 'Watching the pretty ladies go by!!' Fascinated by the events that went on across the road from their window, young Andrew asked his Dad "What are the pretty ladies waiting for?" "Their husbands" his daddy would reply. "How come they keep changing their husbands?" Came the questionable reply. Chris was pleased to move away from there, before her sons education in life study got out of hand!!!!!

THE VISIT

The following year as the daffodils were in full bloom, Jenny returned to English shores for a holiday after an absence of ten years. Phyl and Ern could sense their daughters eagerness in the many letters they exchanged. They had been content with the letters and tapes informing them of the progress of the entire family. How the grand childrens lives were shaping up, what they did for a living, Jenny wrote about it all. They loved the letter that told about Dereks plans to Marry Cathy Wardman on October the 20th 1984, he was happy and in love, that was all they wanted to know. Cathy had connections in England from grandparents, most Australians did, and they felt that maybe they would see Derek again one day. Phyl and Ern talked about a big reunion, if they could get all the family in one part of the world at one time, well maybe it would happen if one wished hard enough.

Peter and Jenny had purchased a home high in the hills in Mundaring in Western Australia, and she seemed contented at last. Her boys were now young men, so they had planned a mammoth trip lasting three months, taking in most of Europe and finally a two week break in a cottage in Lamerton, near Tavistock.

It was to be the first of many tug-of-love journeys that Phyl and Ern would experience with Jenny. At this moment in time, they were just excited at the prospect of seeing her again. Peter had wanted to see so much as this was his first visit overseas away from Australia. He marveled at the history of it all. He had family on his own fathers side to visit in Wales, and Jenny had friends in Scotland. But Ern guessed that she would have been perfectly happy to have spent more time in the Westcountry with them.

They had arrived from Australia and flew directly to Amsterdam, then on to Paris and Italy and Switzerland, postcards arrived from every destination. They were too numerous to mention by the time they put in a personal appearance. 'Woodbine Cottage' at Lamerton, had all the qualities of a country cottage that anyone could dream of. Diane had booked it, and all the gang enjoyed visiting there. All too soon, it was time for them to return to Australia, and on the flight back, Jenny made a silent vow to return.

Phyl and Ern had held each other for comfort as they watched their youngest daughter walk out of their lives once more.

The following year Ern lost his dear sister Jessie. She died on the 5th January 1985. He informed everyone in England, and then rang the family in Australia to impart the sad news because he knew that Jessie had been the favourite Aunty, with a heart of gold and feet that took her places. She had gypsy in her soul, and it was often discovered if you visited, that Uncle Frank, Jessie's husband would think she was out the kitchen making tea, when really she had taken off to Paignton to play Bingo. She wouldn't even stop to change her clothes, and many a time, she just boarded the coach with her slippers on. That was Aunt

Jess and everyone loved her for it. She was the female opposite to Ernie, her family came first and she would sacrifice anything for them. But she was gone now and her children would miss her forever.

Mum & Dad 25th Wedding Anniversary

THE GOLDEN YEAR

Fifty years of togetherness was to be celebrated in August 1986. Plans were underway all around the globe. Derek had married his Australian girlfriend Cathy, who had given him a son. Luke Benjamen who was born 6th November 1985, as he entered the world, he would have been totally unaware of the role he would play the following year, when at just ten months he travelled half way around the world with his Mum and Dad to celebrate his Grand-parents Golden Wedding Anniversary. Jenny experienced a few tussles with Peter when she told him of her intention of going to England for this special event, but she went anyway. Jens two eldest sons Robbie and Trevor were saving hard, but when the time came to book, it was Trevor who could afford the trip. So the party from DOWN UNDER flew British Airways to London.

Dianes airport skirt got another airing, and there was lots to catch up on as they journeyed back to Plymouth. Brian had hired a mini-bus to collect everyone, and when he arrived at Heathrow, he momentarily lost his sense of direction and drove through the gate that took him onto the start of the runway. When he saw some men waving frantically at him, he realised what he had done, he turned around only to discover that he had almost been level with **Concorde'** as it was about to take off! This brought hoots of laughter from everyone.

A cottage had been selected and booked at Whitchurch for the family from Australia. Phyl and Ern visited whilst plans for the party were nearing completion. It was a nice little cottage close to the Moors, Cathy and Derek could put Luke in his pushchair and walk to the village across the field next to the church, it was a lovely holiday and Dereks first time back since 1978.

Jenny Edwards

The day dawned magnificently on the 22nd August 1986. Diane was to host the party at her home in Carfrae, Michael had spruced up the garden, and the girls hung banners everywhere. Diane prepared a whole Salmon for the centre of the buffet. A cake was made by Michelle, and decorated in pale gold, it put the finishing touch. Jenny made one of her Dads favourites, a plate of Pork Brawn, Chris made a pastry dish, she made lovely pastry, and Cathy made an Australian specialty, so there was something for everyones palette'. With plenty of food, and a few bottle of bubbly, surrounded by their family, it was a grand day, even grand enough for Ern to acknowledge the '**OUTSIDERS**'. Photos were snapped under the banner which announced HAPPY 50TH ANNIVERSARY.

Then there was the Christmas in September. Brian and Chris at this time had a house at Eggbuckland, and it was decided that Christmas would be created inside these walls. It was far better than 'Real' Christmas celebrations had been for all of them for several years. They were all together, and the little things could be savoured. From the succulent turkey and trimmings to the pudding that was flamed to great applause and effect. Derek and Brian shared the role of the giving out of the presents, Ern and Phyl sat back and watched as their children re-enacted Christmas past. It was the most wonderful day.

The dustman got an even bigger surprise when he had to cart away the Christmas tree a few days later!!!!what? in September?

During this happy holiday, Trevor met the young girl who was destined to become his wife. She lived at Gunnislake and was a friend of his cousin Jane. Although the plan was to just enjoy each others company for the duration of the holiday, Trevor knew when he boarded the plane at Heathrow with his mum to return to Australia, that he would come back for Michelle one day. Ern and Phyl had the pleasure of Derek, Cathy and baby Luke for a further two weeks as they had decided to stay longer. Jenny had to get back for work, she was the secretary to the Administrator at Swan District Hospital and her months holiday was over. and Trevor had to get back home to return to work as well.

Two weeks later it was time for farewells yet again, this time not just a son but a dear grandson that they were just beginning to come to know. The kisses and hugs would have to last them all a long time. Derek, Cathy and Luke flew back by British Airways and life went on its merry way once more.

How the years flew by after that. Ern still would not admit the fact that he was getting on! Phyl was still trying to convince him that she was capable of much more around the house than he would let her do, but he would not hear of it, and he could be quite stubborn at times, and Phyl knew this only too well.

His favourite job was feeding the many birds that came down to take advantage of his home made bird bath. The Robin was a regular visitor, and the birds whistled louder when they spotted Ernie with scraps.

Sundays was spring clean day, he turned everything out, and vacuumed the entire house, Phyl would follow behind with the duster. Every day during the week, when the chores were completed, Ernie washed, shaved and changed into good clothes. Complete with trilby or deer stalker hat, he would walk down the Square. Sometimes with Phyl and sometimes alone. Meeting people along the way, stopping for a chat, putting a bet on a 'SURE THING' in the three thirty or just putting some humour into the day for the young shop assistants. He could get them all going, they liked old Mr Johns. When the shopping was done, he would come back up the hill and home to Phyl, who would have a tray of tea ready and waiting, she would then listen to his exploits or grumbles about what the Council have, or have not done!!!! It was par for the course.

The summers were spent out the back garden getting browned off, planting or removing seasonal flowers. The Autumn would bring the grumble of "Not all those leaves to sweep away again?" But he did it anyway, he just liked to throw in the odd grumble here and there to give life some variety. He took on the job of cutting the lawns and clearing up for some of the residents who found it all too much. Ernie felt it was his duty especially for the widows, he could give his usual patter to a different audience.

If the role was reversed however, well, that was a different story. He was, and always had been, a jealous man. Phyl could not invite a tradesman into their home, for a harmless cup of tea. He said, he knew what men were like, and she had to promise him, that if anything happened to him, she was not to let any of the men who lived in the street into her house. He assured her, this was for her own safety.

Christmas celebrations these days were alternatively spent at Diane and Michaels house or Brian and Chris's, they always seemed to know whose turn it was. Christmas Day for everyone was enjoyed with their own immediate family, but Boxing Day was the traditional 'Get Together' day. There was always the special things done by them all that would delight Mum and Dad. Children from both sides would entertain, and plan funny presents for Grandad who always put on a good acceptance speech..... like "Unaccustomed as I am to public speaking"........ etc. etc.

The long distance phone call from Australia to link them together, would halt proceedings, and when the festive messages were given and received, the receiver was placed back on the hook at both ends, and cause for refilling glasses and raising them with a toast to absent family was called for in both extremities of the world.

The New Year arrived and heralded hope and prosperity for all. They entered 1987 with much anticipation. Ernie was now in his seventy-fifth year, and Phylis in her seventy-first. Their Autumn years together. The boxes of hankys were certainly piling up. Phyl would smile a familiar smile, because regular as clockwork the box of pretty hankies would be dropped in her lap with a quick retort like "Er yar Till" or "I bet you thought I forgot, didn't ya?"

Trevor kept his word and returned to England from Australia in April 87', to continue his courtship of Michelle Brooks. They visited Trevs Grandad and Nanny at Chard Road many times and enjoyed a good relationship with both of them. Grandad would hear the knock on the door and sheepishly open it half way and say "Not today, thank you!" And then promptly close it again. It was always laughingly received as one of Grandads jokes. Corny or otherwise, Grandad always had a joke. If he saw a cat he would always say "Lets open him up and see how much is in the kitty?"

Trevor with his amiable positive nature quickly found employment for the summer with a Quarry Company in Gunnislake, Cornwall. And a small caravan for accommodation, just over the field from Aunty Di, he was assured of a good feed when he needed it. He had decided that he would ask Michelle to marry him and return to Australia, so they could set up home there.

She accepted his proposal and they got engaged in August. It had been a very wet summer, and many times Michelle had helped Trevor to get his unreliable Datsun Car up the muddy lane from the Caravan Park, so he could get to work. It had worn brakes, but they only worried about that going down Gunnislake Hill.!! Trevor told Michelle of the wonderful warm sunny days that she would enjoy when they moved back to Australia, she couldn't wait.

Ern and Phyl had watched as their own Children had grown up. Now it was their grandchildrens turn, walking the given paths of their chosen destiny.

They attended their grandson Trevor's wedding to Michelle in Plymouth in October of the same year. And just a few weeks later they were the excited recipients of the news of the birth of their very first GREAT-GRANDCHILD. Melissa Louise came into the world prematurely on November 8th 1987. It was Jenny's first grandchild from Shaun and Kelsey. The baby was born in Perth, Western Australia.

Trevor and Michelle, flew back to Australia and a new life together in December, taking with them the good wishes from the English Contingent. Young Michelle was leaving behind a Mum, a Dad and four sisters.

Once more with everyone back 'Down Under' and the English side of the family busy about their work, things reverted almost back to normal. Brian was now not only a builder, but a good stonemason as well. He had the same sincerity and warmth as his Dad, but he knew a good quote when he saw it. Decorative fire places were the thing, and Brians use of natural stone was very artistic. Ern was pleased with the results Bri achieved, he made use of a bit of left over cement one day to create a rustic bird bath, which he put on the sawn off base of an old tree out the back garden. Not quite the job Brian would have done, but everyone knew Ernie was a hammer and six inch nail man, but his heart was in the right place, and he did something for the birds that he loved.

DOWN UNDER, things were far from normal, by the end of 1988, Jenny had separated from Peter; She did not break the news to her parents until the following February.

She simply tried to spare them the worry in their Autumn years.

Ern was pleased, when just three months later, Jen decided to come home to England to be with her parents for a while, just a holiday was all she planned. But you have all heard of the Johnsy 'Change of plan'. The boys were all independent young men and did not live at home anymore, so there was no rush.

Now in his 77th year, Ernie was still eager to take Jenny with him on his daily walks up through higher St. Budeaux, he showed her the new road, and the fly-over, new age technology to Ernie. They walked on through to Higher St. Budeaux Parish Church, the grounds looked pretty in the spring sunshine. He made it quite clear to his younger daughter as they walked and talked, that if anything happened to him, he had taken out an agreement with Earls, the Funeral Directors and everything was paid for. Jenny was stunned at such a revelation, but he assured her that he had had the same conversation with her sister and brother. They walked back home, for a cuppa, Ernie happy to have got it off his chest, and Jenny concerned in case he wasn't telling her everything.

The first place they went when Jen hired 'Wheels' was Plym Bridge, they walked to the river through the bluebells, what a sight, Ernie sat amongst them so Jen could air her camera, and then they changed places.They talked of the many lovely memories of their childhood days out at Plym Valley. The river was still rushing along as it does with the spring tides. They found the tree where they had camped when the whole gang was much younger. Phyl was suffering from a bad back at the time, so she stayed at home, and Ernie took the brood and some extras out to Plym Bridge to camp. The tent was fine until in the dead of night, it started to thunder, and the sky lit up with sheet lightning. Camping under the tree was not such a great idea. They laughed together as the memory of them all shrouded in blankets were led out of the field and away from the trees and up to the old disused train station. The shelter had a concrete floor, so Ernie knew they would be safe there. But no one slept, and every now and again, they would wake their cousin David, who seemed to be the only one sleeping, and jokingly ask him if he wanted to buy a battleship!!!!!Why you may ask? I have no idea, but it brought forth huge giggling sessions. Ern and Jenny took great delight in finding the spot where the station shelter used to be, it was all demolished by then of course and the train line, hardly visible through the weeds, that too was now unused. It was nice to be able to relive the old times.

Having the car, gave Jenny the freedom she thrived on, and a few weeks later, their two daughters, now in their early fourties took off to discover Wales.

Ern and Phyl had never concerned themselves with Jennys driving habits when she lived in Australia, but now she was home they started treating her like their teenage daughter once more. So when Diane and Jenny under-estimated their time of arrival home from Wales the following week, Ern got in a flat spin. From a phone call he had received from them when they reached Bath, near Bristol, he did a rough estimate and expected to see them around four o'clock.

He was frantic when they walked in the door at eight o'clock that night. He blamed Diana for being irresponsible. The two women stood with unbelieving ears listening to their father seriously chastising both of them, like never before. He was still their Father!

Jen and Diane, later confessed, when they were alone that they had found the whole incident quite amusing, and Diane said "I knew it would be my fault!"

Dianes Husband Michael, wasn't in the least perturbed, knowing full well that they had got side tracked somewhere in a shop or turned left. A habit they had. They were born to shop and were dedicated browsers when it came to a row of shops.

Forgiven once more, they made plans for a picnic out at Plym Bridge, and the inevitable game of cricket. It was like the old days except that this day was captured on video film, to be relived at any time. The summer months were glorious. Phyl and Ern did their best to bring Jenny back into the fold, she decided to extend the holiday and wrote to her boss in Australia to ask for three months leave without pay. Diane found her a part-time job behind the bar at St. Mellion, but the days of catering had been long gone for Jenny, who was now a Full-time Secretary. With Di's help she got back into the swing of things again and the sisters enjoyed each others company renewing a bond that had never really been severed. After living at 54 Chard Road, St. Budeaux with Mum and Dad for a month, she moved in with Diane and Michael for the duration of the summer, sharing a bedroom with Michelle. They talked well into the night about Michelles romance with the chef at St. Mellion, Shaun Hicks. The stars in the heavens needed a bit of a boost, and the late night chats and advice brought about plans for an engagement. Love put a sparkle in Michelles eyes. She took her Fiancee to see Nanny and Granddad, and produced the ring which was to be put on her finger at the engagement party. The night was a huge success, it was held down at The Tamar Valley Social Club over looking the river Tamar, a lovely position and Brians local. Bri had done lots of work at the club, and held a variety of positions on the committee. His planning for club members to go to the German Beerfest were notoriously successful. Having lived in Germany, Bri was the ideal guide, and his natural enthusiasm made him the perfect choice for Entertainments Manager.

The whole family was getting very transient by the time plans were hatched over cups of tea for Brian and Diane to go on holiday to Australia, with Jenny, when she returned there in late August. The two brothers and two sisters would have their reunion **TOGETHER**.

August was fast approaching. Phyl and Ern would be celebrating their fifty-third Wedding Anniversary. They had always gone somewhere together, but this year, at Erns suggestion, they invited Jen and Di to share it with them.

The girls hatched plans of their own, they would give their parents a day to remember. Flowers were purchased, for a bouquet and buttonholes for the four of them. With the camera at the ready and a white car decorated with **"JUST MARRIED 53 YEARS"** they all set off.

The first stop was Charles Church, or the remains of it, for a photo call, then they motored on to Ringmore, near Challaborough, to a pub called '**JOURNEYS END**'. They had lunch in the conservatory over looking the back garden. It brought memories flooding back of happy childhood days sitting on furniture made from beer barrels, eating crisps and drinking cider.

Another photo call at the small church on the top of the hill at Ringmore and off they went again, this time to Paignton. Phyl and Ern had previously enjoyed a visit to 'SINGERS', it was a large country estate. The magnificent building housed all the old Singer Sewing Machines from way back, complimented with the most wonderful back drop of oil paintings on huge canvas's. The marble staircase just inside the entrance made you wish you were wearing a long flowing gown, so you could glide gracefully down the wide steps. It had been the focal point of many old movies. Phyl and Ern had enjoyed the visit last time and they wanted to share the enjoyment with their daughters. The experience was not wasted.

Saturation point was reached with the house and its many treasures. So they looked for the nearest exit to enjoy the rest of the afternoon sunshine in the grounds. Not to be beaten, Ernie spotted an 18 hole mini-golf game and suggested they compete. With Phyl settled comfortably on a bench, and a wager on the side, the three intrepid players set about the task of out-putting each other. The first few holes were played according to the rules, but Ernie tired of the rules rapidly and a little slight of hand when no one was looking, put the ball in a much more convenient position, to secure a great putt!! Phyl clapped, and the girls looked at one another and made a silent pact, to let Dad win or they wouldn't hear the end of it. A cool refreshing Ice cream wound up the day. They drove home happy, tired and totally thrilled with the whole adventure.

In August, after a farewell cuppa, Phyl and Ern excitedly waved the trio on its way for the first leg of the journey 'DOWN UNDER'. Jenny had broken the news that her new Friendship with John, One of the Managers at St. Mellion was worth furthering and she would possibly be returning to England again. This was cause for celebration.

With their lucky chickens (lucky charms) clutched tightly in the palm of their hands, the trio took off from Heathrow Airport bound for exotic destinations. The first being Kuala Lumpur (K.L.) where the tastes, sounds, and smells of Malaysia were savoured and written about on many a glossy postcard. Their parents received each card with delight. Bri wrote to Chris, he missed her already. Di wrote to Mike, reminding him of what food was in the freezer and sending her love. Then a card to her girls telling them of the wonderful drinks served up by the pool, high glasses full of exotic fruit and colourful cocktails, topped with a fresh orchid every time. The pool at the hotel was crystal clear and blue, and the whole wonderful place was unashamedly elegant. They enjoyed the warm tropical night air, eating in a restaurant under the stars, and a Malaysian Night Club, not a moment was wasted for this adventurous lot! The Johnsys abroad!!!!

There was now temporarily, no direct descendents, resident on English soil.

By the end of 1989, Brian and Diane had completed their holiday and come back loaded with souvenirs. Jenny followed later.

It was a heartrending parting for Jenny, leaving, not only four sons and their partners, but a two year old grand-daughter Melissa. She had sold up her possessions in Australia and took over an English pub in Falmouth, Cornwall.. This was the testing time for her relationship with John. Christmas in the pub trade is always busy and Phyl and Ern did not see as much of Jenny as they had first hoped. Ern always intended to visit the pub, but the closest he got to Cornwall that year was a Sunday visit with Phyl to the cottage in Landrake where Jenny lived until they moved to Falmouth, They had all enjoyed a cooked lunch and the chance to roast chestnuts on the open fire. Not many places had open fires these days, so this was a rare treat. Ernie was good at roasting chestnuts, he timed them perfectly and removed the shovel from the hot coals at just the right moment, when the nuts would be popping out of their shells.

Phyl experienced many days when Ernie, now thinner with age would shake so badly, he found small jobs horrendous, and using a screwdriver nigh on impossible. In the old days, he had enjoyed a game of EUCHRE or KNAPP with Bri down the pub, but not anymore, he couldn't hold his hand steady for long enough to shuffle a deck of cards. Unbeaten and undeterred, he still got the shopping in and did his chores, whilst humouring Phyl. Still The Great Provider!

Having to admit he needed a hearing aid was one of the worst moments in his life, but his embarrassment subsided when he saw it was just a small device that sat neatly behind the ear. Years of toying with the thing would make it eminate a shrill whistle and he would tell Phyl that "He had it on the wrong channel".

In their quiet hours he prepared Phyl for the ultimate inevitable. He bought her a cuddly teddy bear, just in case she had nothing to cuddle when he wasn't there. He talked finance, and when she found him taking pills that she knew nothing about, she would question him, he would smile and look deep into her eyes and cheekily tap the side of his nose and say "Never you mind".

But in April of 1990 everybody minded when he went on a journey where no one could follow. It was the end of an era, the end of a couple. The beginning of a single existence for Phyl, and she hated it. She fought hard, but it was no use; He had returned home from shopping with Phyl, the day after Easter Monday,1990. He had seemed slower and was lagging behind. Early that day he had chatted on the phone with Jenny, who was preparing to fly out the next day for Australia for her youngest son Raymonds wedding to Lisa Hatcher in Perth, Western Australia. There was much to chat about, on her return she would bring Shaun, Kelsey and their Great Grand-daughter Melissa with her. They would meet for the first time. He knew he wouldn't see Jen before the flight so he jokingly said "Do me a favour, don't get out of the plane before it lands?" they both laughed and hung up the receiver. It was the last words they would ever exchange. By 11.30am. he had struggled up the hill with bags of shopping. Coop were giving away double stamps, so extra provisions were bought, even though a siege was not expected. They put the key in the door and he dropped the bags on the kitchen table saying "I can't do this anymore". Phyl was worried, she had never seen him like this before. She put the kettle on, but he had already collapsed before reaching the bathroom. Panic set in, but she found the presence of mind to pull the emergency cord to summon help. All the old peoples bungalows were fitted with these devices. But Ernie didn't wait around for an ambulance, he was gone. By twelve noon on the 17th April 1990 he checked out, and whatever you believe, which is infinitely personal to each individual, I am the one writing this story of the life and times of my Mum and Dad, and it brings me comfort to believe that on another plain, that is unknown to us all until our fate decrees, there must have been a wonderful reunion. He would meet up with everyone who had gone before him.

It was bluebell time when he left us, and each year when they bloom in profusion and taint the air with their blossom, we are all grateful in our own way to have known him, and to have been part of him and his story. The Greatest Provider. Bless you Always Dad.

Phyl still lives in the neat little bungalow, doing most things for herself. She has shown more courage than she was given credit for, and although it is obvious she misses her lifetime partner very much, she still enjoys family moments and news of the ever increasing family tree.

Diane and Michael are now grand-parents, with the birth of Charlotte May, the first child for Michelle and Shaun. Jenny has two grandchildren, Shaun and Kelseys children, Melissa and Belinda, and twins are expected later this year with Robert and Margie. We are led to believe this will be twins?. How the family will celebrate at Robbie being a Father!

There are lots of empty spaces on this family tree, just waiting for the next generation to fill them.

This story and its main characters take pride of place on the top branches, where the birds sing the sweetest.

1989 Family Photo in a Bluebell Wood

L-R Back: Jenny–Brian–Diane
L-R Front: Mum (Phylis) Dad (Ernie)

Dad in a Bluebell Patch—Plym Valley.